NEXT-LEVEL
BASS
FISHING

INNOVATIVE TECHNIQUES THAT HAVE ELEVATED THE WORLD'S BEST ANGLERS TO THE TOP

JOE KINNISON

Skyhorse Publishing

Skyhorse Publishing books may be purchased in bulk at special discounts for sales promotion, corporate gifts, fund-raising, or educational purposes. Special editions can also be created to specifications. For details, contact the Special Sales Department, Skyhorse Publishing, 307 West 36th Street, 11th Floor, New York, NY 10018 or info@skyhorsepublishing.com.

Skyhorse® and Skyhorse Publishing® are registered trademarks of Skyhorse Publishing, Inc.®, a Delaware corporation.

Visit our website at www.skyhorsepublishing.com.

10 9 8 7 6 5 4 3 2

Library of Congress Cataloging-in-Publication Data is available on file.

Cover design by Kai Texel
Cover image by Getty Images

ISBN: 978-1-5107-6685-3
Ebook ISBN: 978-1-5107-6688-4

Printed in China

To Colleen, Matt, Ben, and Lily for fielding the questions, finding the typos, and encouraging the effort.

Contents

Prologue

Young or old, one's first catch is a memory. Attracting a living thing to your bait is an energy rush. Fighting for control along a thin line pits man against nature. Hoisting a slippery, wiggling water-dweller to the shore brings a feeling of both accomplishment and profound respect for the animal. It does not seem to matter whether you return the fish to the water or keep it for a meal, most people remember their first catch with sense of wonderment.

A first fish need not be spectacular, though some are. The fish could be a tiny bluegill lifted through the slats of a dock. A heavy catfish could have cruised the shoreline to discover your hot dog cutting. An aggressive bass might have inhaled a silvery piece of metal fluttering in the middle of a pond.

Many first fish are hooked with worms, corn kernels, or lunch meats. Catching one with an artificial lure is even more profound. One wonders how this creature can mistake a plastic chunk or a spinning blade for a real fish. You have coaxed the bite and won the fight. You cannot wait to have that experience again.

Second fishing memories often go to a perfect fishing day. It is that one day when you were in the right place and you had the right lure. It seemed like every cast brought in a new fish. You may have caught 10. You may have caught 40. It was constant action. You live in anticipation of another day where you slay the bass.

If not a prolific fishing day, your memory may be of a trophy catch. Those who have caught a lunker know they have experienced a force. The older fish know a few tactics. They can rush or thrash or dive. The fish and the angler are more evenly matched.

ENTHUSIASM

Fishing experiences make memories. They provide rites of passage. They foster essential skills. Some create social bonds. The sport of fishing has been a passion of mine for two decades.

About 40 days per year, I can be found reeling in a bass. I prefer fishing for largemouth. They get big. They fight. Sometimes they perform aerial stunts. Most of this book is oriented toward the largemouth family of the bass species. However, smallmouth, spotted bass, and stripers get a nod.

Prior to starting research for this book, I thought fishing 40 days per year made me an active angler. I could not have been more wrong. Thousands of people fish more than twice that often. Talk about passion.

My wife and friends may disagree, but the numbers suggest that a softer word than "passion" is needed. Let's say that I am an enthusiastic fisherman. I participate in a fishing club, where we build fishing habitats, stock lakes, and hold contests. I have won a few local tournaments.

With decades of experience as an involved but amateur angler, I think it can be hard to isolate a reason why one angler catches more fish than another. "Fishing's not that hard,"[1] indicates a prominent sitcom. Yet, something distinguishes a professional angler from a bass club guy like me.

That something is significant. I see a chasm between myself and anglers on the professional tours. In my circles, we call a largemouth bass larger than five pounds a "lunker." In a good year, I will catch one or two of them. Professionals catch five most fishing days. Clearly, a difference exists.

The temptation is to say it is something material, like better gear or longer experience. It is not the gear. Gear actually has a downside: complexity. It can be hard to solve the multifaceted problem of delivering the right bait with the right rig under the right conditions. I have had opportunities to fish with some accomplished St. Louis-area anglers. I was not the only one who, for fear of embarrassment, has hidden from public view

---

1   "Telethon." *Parks and Recreation*. Season 2, Episode 21. May 10, 2010.

a spinning reel seated on a casting rod. The ability to sort through all of the gear could differentiate good from great anglers, I guess.

What if it is technology? As it is in every other endeavor, technology is changing fishing. From fielding frequent questions, I can tell you that the amateur crowd still struggles to read side-image sonar. It took me hours on the water and repeated YouTube videos to become passably adequate myself. Just when I had become proficient with that tool, 360-degree sonars were released. It will not be long until we can measure the vital signs of a suspending bass using electronics.

As a bass fishing enthusiast, none of these equipment reasons are satisfying. Experience does not completely add up either. I can see that an angler with 100 annual outings may outfish someone who goes 10 times, but 40 times? At some point, the degree of separation has to narrow. No, being a good bass angler must be explained by something other than gear and experience.

A SPORT FOR OUR TIMES

While I was gathering information to explain what makes a pro able to assemble big stringers of fish, bass fishing experienced a rush of new anglers. The pandemic, while an awful health threat, appears to have stimulated the sport. In a normal year, seven million people discover or rediscover fishing. It was far more than that in 2020. Lakes and rivers were crowded with boats, as boat sales advanced by double-digit percentages. Tackle shops saw empty shelves. Fishing license sales rose 40 percent in some states. In past years, I would share the dawn on my home lake with one or two other anglers. This year, the average was four times that figure.

Not only was my lake full, but also the surge of new anglers showed up countrywide. While most other travel was suspended, fishing tourism thrived. Some of America's famous bass lakes are in comfortably remote locations. An automobile provides the most convenient access, so flights can be avoided. Best of all, many of the lakes are served by welcoming small towns.

To the extent that professional anglers accrue a relative benefit from visiting prominent bass fishing venues, the amateurs are catching up.

For the new fishing tourists, sections of this book have something of a travel log. To those who have not yet discovered these outposts, I suggest lodging, food, guide services, and a few sights. My wife likes to travel, so my approach to these locations was to try to find places where she would enjoy spending time while I fish. Your tastes may differ.

Regarding the lakes and rivers in this book, they are among the nation's best bass locales. Fair-minded people can argue over which bass lakes are the very best. The most productive waters change over time. Personal fishing style and relative proximity factor into most anglers' equations. Professional anglers have recommended the lakes and rivers in this book. I am willing to take their word for it.

For the fisheries sampled, topographic maps illustrate snippets of underwater terrain. The maps become dated quickly. Water levels change. Lakes sediment. Current moves structures around. The intent of the maps is to highlight areas where natural contours are favorable for largemouth bass. The maps are meant only as a starting point for visiting amateurs.

Experience on the big bass lakes might be emerging as a less decisive difference between bass clubbers and pro anglers. The knowledge gap we identified earlier need not be persistent. So, why do the pros keep catching multiple big fish when I do not?

While many of us were escaping lockdowns to lakes and rivers, the professional fishing tours were suspended. During those months, some professional anglers gave freely of their time to help this enthusiast try to sustain the recent broadening of the sport. I admire their willingness to mentor the many people getting their first taste of bass angling.

Over the course of many conversations, emails, and texts, I came to a realization. Although the technical information these anglers relayed was detailed and insightful, it may not be determinative. The important difference, the next-level gradient, seemed not to be what tips these anglers provided. Instead, it turned out to be the personal qualities they possess.

To my eye, anglers who reach the next level have several characteristics in common. They are structured; they are sensory; they are versatile; they are coachable; and they are original. While that list of qualities may be daunting to consider instilling in yourself, I have good news. Each person's capabilities in these areas can be enriched, and this book shows you how.

Can better organization skills make you a better angler? Yes. They represent the difference between throwing a bait and fishing intentionally. Is sense acuity something that can be tuned? Absolutely. You will not believe the natural details that you are missing.

For the 38 million people who regularly wet a line and the millions who started this year, you can ascend to the next level of angling. Catching more fish and bigger fish is an attainable goal. However, the answers are not found in a tackle shop or on a waterfront. Next-level angling requires personal development. Read on to improve your fishing and to understand what makes a pro a pro.

CHAPTER I
Vice:
A moral fault or failing.[1]

T wo anglers cast the same lures into the same lake. One catches more fish than the other. Culturally, people seem to account for this difference by assigning a long list of vices to the more successful angler. Good anglers are lucky. They have poor temperament. The results were bought, not earned. If not these causes, the angler must have engaged in outright deception.

For the angler with the bigger stringer of fish, a first premise is that luck must have determined the outcome. You have no doubt met an angler who seems to be unusually fortunate. I am speaking of the type of person who walks out on the dock where you have been casting determinedly and catches a fish the moment their line hits the water. You know the ones. The grade schooler outfitted with the stick, twine, and pop-top can rigging. Many of us have had this experience. We tell ourselves that these people have a knack for fishing. Pure chance seems to be a more palatable explanation than slightly better cast placement or a more suitably paced retrieve.

If it is not luck that defines the prolific angler, then doubters claim that it must be temperament. One of the earliest theories of personality type identified four classical temperaments. People could be characterized as choleric, sanguine, melancholic, phlegmatic, or a combination

---

1   Retrieved November 1, 2020, from https://www.merriam-webster.com/dictionary /vice

of two traits. Each of these personality types has positive and negative attributes. However, the phlegmatic temperament has some of the least aspirational aspects. The derogatory usage of "phlegmatic" classifies a person as lazy, passive, and patient to a fault. To use the ancient term as a fishing skeptic, good anglers must be phlegmatic.

When people who do not enjoy fishing list faults, patience is the quality most attributed to anglers. The "patience" vision of fishing is an image of an angler sitting in the same place all day waiting for a fish to swim nearby. Relaxing or napping may be good reasons for sitting still. However, sedentary people with a line in the water are not seriously fishing, at least not for bass.

To a bass angler, patience is an insult. The patience narrative presumes that fishing presents no challenge other than standing still. Bad temperament seems a comfortable way to degrade someone who is studiously collecting sensory input from the outdoor environment.

If it is not lamentable patience that defines the successful angler, it must be deception. Fishing lore encourages the notion that an angler fabricates stories, conceals methods, and exaggerates catches. The frustrated are quick to dismiss a large stringer. They claim that it was assembled dishonestly. Certainly, the fish have been tricked. Possibly, other anglers were deceived as well.

Despite fishing success being so maligned, millions of anglers appear at the water's edge to try their luck, indulge their temperament, and practice deception. Fishing has become the second-largest outdoor activity in the United States. It trails only running as an active pastime. Given the high degree of disparagement of anglers, the large number of participants suggests that practitioners must have acquired a thick skin. They overcome the ongoing assault on their character traits.

Fishing is a sport filled with passionate practitioners. The number of enthusiasts who fish more than 100 times per year reaches into the six digits. If the detractors who seem to define the sport are correct, this is a large, growing, and somewhat organized group of ne'er-do-wells: derelicts who frequently produce large stringers of bass. Worse, the derelicts have organized. Across the country, bass clubs are emerging and thriving. The really reprehensible anglers populate two top-level professional fishing tours.

Since fishing antagonists define much of the sport, one wonders how avid anglers would represent themselves if given the chance. As it turns out, these anglers do themselves no favors in explaining fishing success. Many define the sport in terms of what can be purchased.

The most celebrated anglers collect specialized tools and components. They are differentiated by their custom baits. They seem to assume the mantra that superior gear defines fishing success. Dozens of rods and reels are proof of attainment.

While these are nice collections, the investment required is unreachable for many and unnecessary for most. Not much evidence ties spending with fishing success. In fact, the average angler spends less than $60 per year on fishing supplies. Yuppies with new boats and expensive rods often return to the dock with empty live wells.

With emphasis on gear, bass fishing can become about as outdoorsy as NASCAR racing. Yes, fishing occurs in a natural setting, but anglers surround themselves with products and technologies of all sorts. They outfit themselves in wide-brimmed hats, polarized glasses, wicking fabrics, gloves, and face coverings. Some anglers have precious little exposure to the elements. They can go a whole fishing day barely touching water. Instead of improving catch rates, excessive fishing equipment can actually distance the angler from the angling.

As if errors in crediting gear sets was not bad enough, frequent anglers are quick to diminish their own. Even passionate anglers seem to look down upon those with the most experience. Those with dozens of annual outings are condemned as having too much idle time. Anglers who fish in less than ideal conditions are considered zealous. Fishing may be the only sport in which practice is frowned upon.

Neither luck, nor patience, nor deception, nor gear explain the angler who frequently brings home full stringers of fish. Which vices produce such positive results? None. Positive personal qualities are the true determinants of fishing success.

NEXT-LEVEL QUALITIES

Anglers who have elevated themselves into the upper echelons of fishing trace their "luck" to acute sensory skills. Good anglers see things that less accomplished fishermen do not. They may feel a change in the wind or hear a distant bass rush the shore. Some anglers are sensitive to turbidity, and others see shades of color in the water. Sensitive practitioners detect smells above the waterline. A next-level angler will collect sensory inputs and use these stimuli to dictate positioning and presentation. This activity takes concentration, and concentration can be confused with sloth.

Just as luck is more likely sensory skill, the patience myth conceals the opposite truth. Nearly the opposite of the phlegmatic type, bass anglers tend toward the choleric temperament. Most successful anglers are self-starting, analytical, and competitive. Having analyzed conditions and options, they pursue bass with a commitment to method. For example, fan casting a laydown is done in a prescribed pattern. Moreover, Texas-rigged plastic craws are retrieved with near-perfect mimicry of the movement of the creature. If their research suggests that bass will be on main channel ledges, anglers stay disciplined to target that terrain. They measure their results, and they manage their time.

Staying structured and active catches more fish. Few professional anglers are patient. They move from site to site to find fish. They change lures when their first selection is not working well enough. They agitate at the edge of a body of water waiting for the sunrise.

Accusations of deception stem from fishing's lore. The sport has oral traditions, and those forms of communication are a credit to anglers. Mentorship is an important part of the fishing tradition. It is a way that anglers translate biology, legacy, and individual specialties to one another. Jokes and stories make for productive chatter.

While traditions offer important guidance, a spark of originality often makes the ultimate difference. Intuition to make a radical shift in lure colors, or the notion to alternate between spinner baits and swim baits can make the difference between a good fishing day and a great fishing day. The courage to be creative, take chances, and differentiate oneself truly makes an angler next-level. As with any sport, the best athletes mix fundamentals with flair.

INTRODUCTIONS

The world has many methods of identifying the "best" bass anglers. Top 10 finishes are tabulated, and prize money is summed. The sport is even developing its own version of sabermetrics to calculate catch rates and weights. While acknowledging the statistical measures, I was looking for something different. These touring professionals are the best bass anglers at identifying personal traits that produce sustained fishing advantages. Their willingness to reveal these secrets provides a path for amateur anglers to rise to the next level.

Christiana Bradley has participated in seven FLW professional tournaments and 40 Bassmaster events. She has six Top 10 tournament finishes. Statistically, her best year was 2013, where she finished fourth in two separate ABA Bassmaster events. Her top results occurred on the James River and at Douglas Lake. Her fourth-place finish in the 2013 Southern Open was the best performance by a woman at a Bassmaster Open tournament at that time. Christiana's strength as an angler is her focus.

Tyler Carriere returned to competitive fishing in 2014 after a 14-year hiatus. After some warmup tournaments, he achieved success, finishing 11th at the Bass Central Open on Table Rock Lake in 2016. The following year, he produced a series of Top 50 finishes. His scores qualified him for the Bassmaster Elite series. Now in his fourth year on the Elite tour, Tyler consistently makes the weekend cut. He is a methodical angler who can fill his live well from a single stump.

Destin DeMarion has been the second-highest-ranked angler on two separate professional tours. He reached the number two spot in the Phoenix Bass League Northeast tournament series in 2012, and he equaled that result on the Toyota Series, Northern Division, in 2014. After 31 tournaments in those tours, Destin qualified for the Bassmaster Elite series. He has more than 50 starts and five Top 10 finishes in the Elite series. Destin has his own adaptation of power fishing, making him one of the most creative anglers on tour.

Brandon Palaniuk has fished in more than 100 Bassmaster tournaments, and he has finished in the money an incredible 75 times. Brandon is one of the leading money winners on tour. He has qualified for the prestigious Bassmaster Classic nine times. Brandon has five tournament victories including 2020 triumphs at the Elite series tournaments on Lake Champlain and Santee Cooper. He had one outright win (Sam Rayburn) and three other Top 5 finishes to earn the 2017 Bassmaster Angler of the Year award. Brandon's strength as an angler is that he has a particular sense of the physiology of the fish he pursues.

Pam Martin-Wells is the winningest female angler of all-time. In 38 tournament appearances, she posted four wins and 20 Top 10 finishes. She is the leading money winner in the history of the women's tour. Pam is a six-time Ladies Bass Anglers Association Angler of the Year, with her most recent win in 2020. She is the top women's finisher in the history of the Bassmaster Classic, placing 25th in 2010. Pam's versatility may be the best in fishing.

CHAPTER 2

Preparation:
The action or process of making something ready for use or service.[1]

Pam Martin-Wells describes the process of preparing to visit a new body of water by saying, "You have to eliminate water." By that phrasing, she means that particular areas of lakes and rivers can be identified as having a low likelihood of supporting fish. Those areas are ones to avoid.

Eliminating water utilizes modern tools including video footage, satellite images, and sonar maps. Unfavorable terrain and traffic can be isolated from these sources. With the breadth of material available, Pam will begin her study of upcoming lake and river visits months in advance. From the comfort of her home, these tools all can be used to examine bodies of water and pinpoint probable fishing locations.

Using one of Pam's investigation routes, Tyler Carriere does video study prior to launching his boat on a new lake. Archival video exists of past catches on many of the nation's largest bass waters. Available video footage ranges from old fishing show episodes, to YouTube posts, to past tournament footage. In some of these clips, anglers boast of their location. These may or may not be reliable. In others, shoreline landmarks reveal the location of the catch.

---

1   Retrieved November 1, 2020, from https://www.merriam-webster.com/dictionary/preparation

Even though submerged flats, ledges, and humps look alike from the surface, anglers have become proficient at identifying such locations using visible, topographical features. A water tower, a docked boat cover, or a rock formation could give away a site. Recently, a guide working on Lake Tohopekaliga (Lake Toho) in Florida explained that he has to protect his best spots. He takes pictures of the trophy catches by client anglers while lying on the deck of his boat. Aiming the lens upward, he can frame snapshots with only the sky in the background. Despite such concealment efforts, still and video evidence of some of the most productive fishing locations exists. It is in the public domain. Tyler reviews the visuals to locate the best spots.

While Tyler is combing through videos, other anglers make use of Google Earth. Brandon Palaniuk scans satellite images for dark-bottom coves. Changes in the color of the water are visible on most satellite images. Brown patches may be areas with silty, soft bottoms or they may be locations where muddy inflow mixes with main lake water. Either way, bass will likely be attracted to those areas. Prior to launching a bass boat, a visit to these spots would be planned. Much of the surrounding water would be eliminated.

While Brandon Palaniuk uses the eye in the sky to see color changes, Christiana Bradley raises satellite study to another level. Over many years, she has assembled a collection of images of lakes and rivers during times when their regions are experiencing drought conditions.

During droughts, the water frequently recedes below its normal pool. In cases, the surface level can drop 5 to 10 feet. As the water level recedes, shoreline structures become visible. Features normally deep underwater come into view. For example, the area around Colorado's Pueblo Reservoir experienced severe drought conditions during the summer of 2020. During that time, rock formations that are normally submerged became visible to the eye in the sky. Where nothing but blue water was visible six months ago, satellite images show what appear to be white pillars of rock emerging from several coves. Knowing the location of these formations may provide a competitive advantage a few years from now when the lake is back at full pool.

Christiana can fish locations that only she has the space-based intelligence to find.

To a degree, aspiring next-level anglers can reproduce Christiana's collection of drought images. Armed with climate records, an angler can search Google Earth for historic drought photos. While it is possible to collect dated records, assembling more current data can be patient work. Recent images can be as much as six months delayed.

While satellite images can offer some insights, lake maps with underwater topography are increasingly available. The National Oceanic and Atmospheric Association (NOAA), the same people who predict hurricane paths, supply Raster Navigational Charts for many of the coastal fisheries in the USA. Raster describes the grid pattern used to gather sonar data.

While NOAA is state of the art and regularly updated, the agency is not the only source of underwater topographical charts. Fishing electronics manufacturers offer software that shows charting of the bottom structure of many lakes and rivers. Navionics provided many of the maps used in this book. Their ChartViewer software packages start at $150. They are well worth the cost.

While charts are available, some anglers prefer to make their own maps. Doing so requires a tedious process of tracking a boat back and forth across a body of water, a pattern akin to mowing a lawn. Anglers willing to put in the time can create proprietary underwater intelligence. These maps can be installed on many fish finder marine units. An angler willing to put in this work will likely have a significant advantage. However, eliminating water for fishing by first running sonar over every inch takes a serious time commitment.

It was not long ago, within the last two decades, that the best way to navigate a lake would be to acquire a hand-drawn map from a local tackle shop. Kingfisher Maps (www.kfmaps.com) has digitized and waterproofed that heritage. They now provide local knowledge and map panels for eight Southeastern states.

While maps of underwater topography are now attainable, they may not be the full solution for anglers. Not all maps have the gradation

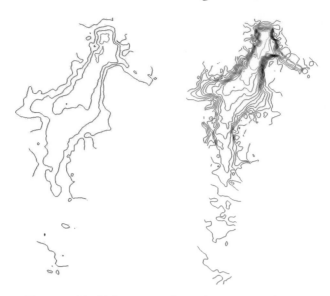

Topographical lake map with 10-foot contour lines.

anglers need. Some show lines for every 10-foot depth change. The graphic above shows a section of a lake using a 10-foot contour interval. The shoreline slope and some underwater humps are visible.

While 10-foot topographic lines are better than nothing, insight into smaller depth changes is preferred. Gradients drawn at six-foot intervals are better, and maps with three-foot depth lines provide the optimal solution for identifying areas likely to hold fish.

Using the narrow three-foot gradients, an angler would start at the shoreline and work outward. The first contour line from the shore is called the scatterpoint. It is the layer at which schools break apart and every fish swims for itself. Areas where scatterpoints are farthest away from the shore are the areas where bass are found at dawn and dusk.

Moving farther out into the body of water, the second place to look for fish is a breakpoint. A breakpoint is identified by finding a series of contour lines in close proximity to each other. These breakpoints represent more rapid depth changes. Bass will congregate at these steeper slopes when moving up and down the water column.

A final target for map orientation is to attempt to locate humps. Humps are usually circular in shape with topographic lines extending in farther circles down into the depths. Bass will dwell near these humps, which provide ready access to both deep and shallow water.

TOOLS

Map study normally occurs off the water, as does equipment maintenance. Protecting equipment has a bigger bearing on fishing success than you might think. An entire day of fishing can be lost to a flat trailer tire, a dead battery, or an overheated outboard motor. Even if the lost time is not a whole day, precious minutes can be lost to something as simple as a preventable line tangle.

Few think of a boat trailer as being a key to fishing. Few consider the boat trailer at all. It is a necessary appendage that many anglers use to launch their boat a few times per year. However, as with most equipment, proper function requires maintenance. Tire pressure checks, the same as those you would perform on your car or truck, improve reliability and mileage. Regular axle grease is necessary to moderate friction. The occasionally submerged electrical connections near the taillights merit regular attention.

Trailer problems are much easier to fix when the trailer is empty. Mobility is easier, and access is better. Adding a thousand-pound boat aboard makes most every repair harder. No one's fishing skill can overcome inability to get the boat to the water.

Trailering gets an angler to the lake. A fully operational boat keeps her there. The functionality of the boat determines how far you go, how fast you go, and what situations you put yourself in on the water. In short, boat reliability determines the extent of the lake or river available to an angler. Especially in bodies of water with regular current, having confidence in your equipment can lessen exposure to some scary situations. So says someone who once nearly got sucked down a spillway.

Even the best-maintained boats break down at times. Professional events have repair stations sponsored by the major boat and motor vendors. Separately, many bass fishing destinations have dockside services. While help may be available, going to one of those stations is not cost-free. A tow can be expensive, and limping to the repair shop can be time-consuming.

It helps to be handy. In one tournament, Christiana Bradley was able to diagnose her own motor problem. Tied up aside a pier, she used her cell phone to order a replacement part. It shipped overnight, and she made the repair in the parking lot. Her do-it-yourself fix saved her tournament.

Keeping the boat at top function may preserve an angler's chances. A particular part of a fishing boat, the live well, may determine the outcome of the weigh-in. Several factors influence how long a fish can thrive in a live well. Water temperature, oxygenation, and the mass of the fish all play a part. In the most general terms, a stringer of five bass can live for five to eight hours in a live well. That duration depends on proper functioning of the filling and circulating pumps, unobstructed hoses, and the lack of bacteria or fungus in the well.

Cleaning occurs shoreside, although next-level anglers may stow a mild detergent aboard. Dawn dishwashing soap is a popular choice. After a wash and a thorough rinsing, a live well is best maintained by keeping the cover off until it dries. Clean and dry surfaces limit bacteria and mold.

Problems with fish thriving in live wells are not always pollution issues. Obstructions infrequently occur when pumps draw water from a fishing area replete with vegetation. Leaves and plants can be suctioned into the tube. Clogs can prevent the water from being refreshed and oxygenated. These clogs can often be cleared with pressure coming from the reverse direction. For live well preservation, another boating essential is a small hand pump. A small hand pump putting pressure against the normal water flow can clear most obstructions.

Dwelling on live well maintenance may sound mundane, but these steps do factor into ultimate success. Destin DeMarion lost a tournament due to a failure of a live well pump. In competitions, dead fish are penalized.

Competitive anglers are not permitted to cull dead fish from their live wells. Even if the angler lands larger bass, a dead fish must be weighted as part of the angler's five-fish stringer. As if that penalty is not bad enough, most tournaments deduct four ounces from the weight of any dead fish. The penalties for accidental fish kills are prohibitive. As such, live well maintenance can be the difference between winning and losing a tournament.

FILAMENTS

Functioning capital equipment enables time on the water, and proper maintenance of fishing line can keep lures in the water for longer. Some types of fishing line develop memory. The winding of the line on the reel will release in a spiral when the line is cast. This spiral, which tightens as it ages, can reduce both casting accuracy and distance by dragging on the eyelets of the rod. Worst of all, the spirals can ultimately turn upon themselves and create a massive tangle colloquially called a bird's nest.

While line memory can be frustrating, line deterioration can be worse. Nature works against fishing line. Prolonged exposure to sunlight degrades most filaments. Nylon monofilament fades in patches and becomes increasingly brittle with UV light exposure. Idle exposure to light and heat degrades fishing line, almost as much as active use. Dragging lures over submerged branches and rocks causes abrasion. As with sunlight degradation, abrasion is detectable. Abraded line will begin to feel rough to an angler's touch, and glass threads may splinter from the main.

Through either exposure or abrasion, fishing line will eventually fail. The point of failure varies, but a line often fails where it is twisted tightly near the knot. Having a line failure with a fish hooked can be devastating to a competitive angler. Tyler Carriere once had a fish that would have made a difference to his total break off in the weeds of Lake Chaplain. Sometimes the bass wins. However, this sort of disappointment can be reduced by frequently replacing fishing line.

Fluorocarbon line is most prone to acquiring memory. It should be replaced twice each fishing season. While fluorocarbon requires the most frequent changes, anglers would be testing their luck with monofilament should they go a full year without replacing that variety. While its alternatives necessitate frequent restringing, braid can last two to five years on a reel spool.

Restringing a fishing reel is a simple process. To begin, old line is unspooled and the knot around the reel spool is cut. With the line spool empty, many anglers disassemble and lubricate the reel. With regular use, most fishing reels have a 10-year life. That timetable can be extended considerably with gear oil applied on a regular basis to the bearings and the gears. Occasionally, an unmaintained bearing will seize during a fishing outing. The reel will begin to grind. A frozen reel is another happenstance that can ruin a fishing day.

With a reel in good condition, new line can be strung by arranging a spool of new fishing line so that the filament winds off the replacement cartridge in a counterclockwise direction. Thread the line through the closest eyelet of the rod to the reel. Run it down the rod to the empty line spool on the reel. Loop the new line around the spool and tie it fast with an arbor knot.

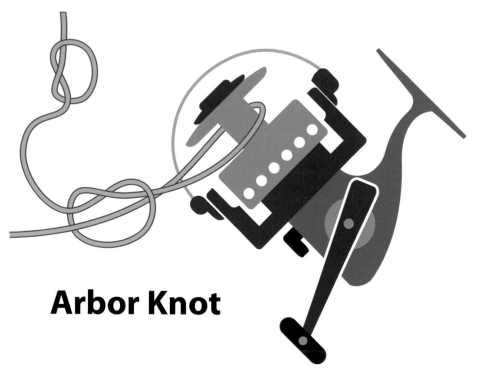

Arbor Knot

Credit: Getty Images

An arbor knot is a simple succession of two overhand knots, one over the incoming line and one at the working end of the string. Once cinched to the reel, trim any remaining excess line past the outward overhand knot. Test the knot security by tugging on the line. With the knot secure, put light tension on the connection between the new line cartridge and the reel and turn the handle to draw line from the cartridge onto the reel. The reel is full when the line is between ⅛ and 1/16 of an inch from the top edge of the line spool.

While it varies by the weight of the line, reels are generally designed to hold 200 yards of string. Few accomplished anglers use that much string in a season. Retying knots and the occasional snag do not consume much. With string being expensive, it is tempting to fill the reel to a level below its line capacity. Yet, underfilling can have performance implications. For example, fishing line can catch against the edge of the spool if the angle of its release is too steep. The remedy is to start filling each reel with braided line. Wrap the braid three times around the spool. Braided line is prone to slipping when tied to a spool with a singular loop. Three loops seems to hold its position. After reeling to load about 100 yards of braid, stop and cut the braided line beyond the first eyelet toward the replacement line spool. Splice the weights and types of line suited for your fishing purpose. For example, tie monofilament to the braid. Use a surgeon's knot or a uni knot.

Substantial cost savings accrue when it is time to update the line. Instead of replacing the entire spool, substitute only the spliced section. Using a braid base, the amount of line to be replaced decreases appreciably.

Preparation for next-level fishing does not end at the reel. Knots connecting the lure to the line require maintenance. Knot failure is the most common reason for losing both lures and fish. Opinion varies about how often to retie the knots holding the baits, but consensus seems to center on renewing knots every fishing day as a base case. Throw the base case out of the window after landing a large fish. After weighing the lunker and taking its picture, retie the lure. Knots should be assessed frequently when fishing heavy cover.

PREPAREDNESS

Tomorrow's temperature will be 89 degrees. The barometric pressure will be rising. Winds gusts up to 25 miles per hour are expected. If this sounds like a basic nightly weather report, you are correct. Anticipating the weather for the next fishing day can mean the difference between successful angling and returning to the dock with an empty live well.

Weather can determine both the location of fish and the utility of lures. With a relatively accurate weather forecast, an advanced angler should have a sense of how the bite might change overnight or through the fishing day. Heavy rains might change tactics to target water movement or muddy water inflows. A passing cold front could guide bait downsizing or increased targeting of shallow coves. Clear skies may drive fish deeper and change lure selection to deeper-diving alternatives. Fish move with weather conditions, and next-level anglers use weather forecasts to anticipate their movements.

The fish are not the only ones impacted by weather. Dealing with weather challenges can distract anglers from their purpose. A rain suit in which you have complete confidence is a next-level essential. Staying dry when the skies open up frees an angler to concentrate on casting and retrieving.

Prior to launching a boat, next-level anglers have examined videos, satellite images, and lake maps. Their tools are in top shape. Live wells are clean and dry. Reels have updated string, and lures are tied with new knots. They are outfitted for the weather. Preparation is the starting point for advancement in fishing.

CHAPTER 3

Structure:
Something arranged in a definite pattern of organization.[1]

Tyler Carriere could see a bass. For a teenager accustomed to drifting the murky Atchafalaya River, actually seeing a water dweller was startling. Visiting his grandmother in Monroe, Louisiana, had its perks. One of those perks was her clear local lake. With the fish down more than eight feet, it was like watching the creature through a set of Coke-bottle glasses.

Tyler stalked the fish from the surface, his eagerness constrained by the dinged but rounded edges of his aluminum boat. When the fish stilled, Tyler reached for his rod and swung a tube bait over the edge of the hull. Dragging loose string from the reel, the tube crashed to the bottom of the lake. The impact startled the bass, and it disappeared into the depths.

Aggravated at missing his chance, Tyler launched himself to a standing position. The force of his brown leather boots against the hull sent ripples from the sides of the boat. He bent the tip of his rod skyward in a fit of teenage angst and ripped the tube up off the bottom. It rose most of the way to the surface. More out of disappointment than intent,

---

1   Retrieved November 1, 2020, from https://www.merriam-webster.com/dictionary /structure

he dropped the rod tip into the water and let the tube flutter back downward.

The tube bait sank only a few feet when his line tightened. The bass reappeared and devoured the lure. The fish swam for open water, taking up the slack and then stripping line from the reel. Tyler regained his grip and fought for control. He guided the fish to the surface, and the bass exploded out of the water. With the fish airborne, Tyler pulled so hard that the animal flattened against the mottled surface of the water. It skimmed like a green smear to the edge of the boat. With the rod and string, he hoisted a monster bass aboard.

As the fish flopped against the ribbed bottom of the boat, Tyler marveled at his prize. Making a few crude measurements, he thought he might have set a new state record. Eventually, he dug out the swallowed tube.

Young Tyler Carriere. Almost a record.

Three hours of weighing and measuring later, the fish proved one pound too light for posterity. While Tyler would not have spurned the record, by that time, he knew that he had done nearly everything wrong. He was visible to the fish. He banged around the boat. He was indelicate with his cast. He gave up on his retrieve. He water skied his catch, and he lifted a nearly 13-pounder into the boat with a 10-pound-test line. He had displayed barely enough skill to land the lunker. He realized in that moment that he needed to raise his angling to the next level.

Luckily, Tyler had ample opportunity to practice. The Atchafalaya River was nearly in the backyard of his childhood home. Tyler could be home from school and afloat on the slow, muddy Mississippi River tributary in no time. Day after day, he fished voids between the tops of hydrilla blooms and the tangles of lily pads. Achieving only modest success amid the thick shoreline mat, he tired of the banks.

He needed to "change it up." Tyler withdrew about 50 feet offshore to the open channel of tannic water. He began casting lures behind standing cypress and tupelo trees, most of which held up a gray drape of Spanish moss. His results quickly improved. Soon, he was patterning fish among offshore trees, stumps, and root balls.

Having found success, he gained confidence. Tyler started lofting alternating lures. With particular fondness, he remembers his first casts of a plastic worm rigged wacky-style. This configuration was next-level stuff for Tyler, and it worked. His fishing progressed so well, he was catching so many, that he felt ready to try to qualify for a fishing tour.

Qualify he did. Tyler earned some early tournament wins. However, not long after his competitive debut, he gave up fishing for a regular paycheck. Fourteen years and two children later, Tyler's wife, Casey, encouraged him to make another attempt at a fishing career. He had kept in fishing shape and maintained his clean-shaven, boyish looks. Swapping soccer dad hoodies for fishing jerseys, he quickly resumed looking the part. With the support of his family ever present, Tyler seldom talks fishing without flashing his yellow and white gold wedding ring.

Though outfitted and supported, a knowledge base consisting of fishing-stained water and heavy cover was insufficient for a national tour, and he wanted to go big. He needed to learn other techniques. Sight fishing, something Christiana Bradley does almost daily, Tyler had accomplished exactly once (sort of) at his grandmother's lake. Likewise, deep water in Louisiana meant five feet deep, not the 50+ foot depths he started to experience when touring the country.

You could not tell by his openmouthed smile and eyebrows arching high in the center, but his first year in his return to competitive fishing was dismal. Military-length hair showed a little gray above his temples, and a continual shifting of weight from one foot to another did clue some distress. He spent a year learning how to read sonar displays.

In his second season, Tyler went for broke, deciding to fish both Bassmaster Open divisions, Central and Northern. Over the course of eight Open tournaments (and 10 others), he elevated himself to a consistent top contender. The results qualified him to join the Bassmaster Elite series in 2018.

In a drawl that translates a smile and hints at Cajun, Tyler reports that the occasional lake still "kicks his ass." Yet, he continues to advance. To date, he has five Top 30 tournament finishes. As he assembles a new set of skills, Carriere posts competitive stringers by saturation casting underwater structure.

HABITAT

Most anglers know that largemouth bass favor structure. The ambush predators select hiding places under logs, behind stumps, and next to rocks. From there, they can rush unsuspecting baitfish. Aiming bait directly at the heart of a structure might catch one fish, but Tyler Carriere's method can fill an entire live well from one brush pile. The trick is to select the right one and fish it methodically.

For starters, not all structure attracts fish. Tyler selects the brush pile that is best located. The cover has to be at the depth preferred by the bass on that given day. For example, a brush pile in 25 feet of water is not likely populated by fish during spawning season. However, a similar form in five feet is a good prospect. In a more linear view of the importance of depth, Tyler reports that bass will only congregate on one set of poles holding up a dock or a pier. It may be the closest set to shore, the middle set, or the deep side edge, but it will seldom be all three. The depth of the structure is paramount.

While location can determine which structure holds fish, the type of cover has an equal influence. Tyler insists that natural material holds more fish than wholly artificial habitats. Some lakes and rivers help take care of themselves by felling the occasional tree from the shore. For bodies of water needing outside help to create fish habitat over time, anglers and resource managers have several options. Common artificial habitats with natural elements span from evergreens wired to a cement block to bamboo cemented into five gallon buckets.

In areas where natural material is lacking or in cases where a more permanent habitat solution is desired, fabricated fish habitats are the answer. Artificial tree assemblies are available from several vendors. Kits can be purchased, assembled, and sunk. For the handy, fake trees can also be constructed by drilling lawn sprinkler tubing through PVC pipe stands. Whether natural or artificial, any structure is better than no structure.

Recent studies show aging lakes having lost places for fish to grow and develop. Responding to these reports, anglers all over the country have been placing natural and constructed trees in major lakes. Resource management agencies often support such efforts by providing materials, holding habitat construction days, and mapping placed structures.

When Tyler is selecting some of this new structure to fish, he proceeds to his target depth and starts by sampling cover made from natural elements. If the environment is target rich, he will concentrate on variations, like gaps between branches or alternating branch lengths. His experience is that fish prefer something unique among submerged features. Gaps create attack vectors.

Next to its location and shape, the age of the cover drives fish presence. Fresh trees often hold fish. The animals seem attracted to the newest greenery. Fish have been known to take up residence below newly fallen trees within hours of water contact. As the greenery dies back over several weeks, algae begins to grow on branches and trunks. That algae attracts more baitfish, and the presence of baitfish later attracts lunkers.

If natural habitats are absent, the next step in Tyler's method is to explore artificial cover. He has regular success fishing dock piering, and he finds fish among fabricated trees. Artificial trees perform the same function as the real ones. They provide darkened corners in which predators can hide. While similar in frame, artificial fish habitats take longer to grow algae and longer to attract aquatic residents. The relative lack of organic matter on the manufactured trees results in a delay between sinking of the structures and the algae bloom. Although artificial habitat takes longer to establish, it lasts for decades once it rests in place. If Tyler can identify aged artificial root wads and trees, he will target those structures.

Finding optimally located, featured, and aged habitat is the starting point. Next-level angling depends on how that cover is harvested. When amateur anglers come upon a fallen tree laying down in the water, they ready a cast to the most attractive junction between trunk and branch. Casting a lure into that ambush point may indeed produce a bass, but it will likely be the only fish caught on that particular structure. The fight between fish and angler will disperse other fish relating to that cover.

Catching one good fish from a structure may not be maximizing the opportunity. Structures that hold fish often hold more than one. However, the fish are not oblivious to a member of their school in distress. It takes a skilled angler to extract several bass from the same water feature. To accomplish the feat, Carriere's method is to fish from the outside in.

Fan casting is a technique of launching casts in the pattern of a semicircular handheld fan. With the target set in the middle of the fan, the angler casts a few feet wide of the believed outer branches of a laydown. The subsequent casts are landed a few feet inward toward the target. The angler continues to work toward the center until reaching the structure itself. Casts continue until the opposite side of the laydown has been probed. Fan casting is an effective method of casting comprehensively around a target.

With a sense of where the outer edges of submerged branches might be, he begins by casting beyond the perimeter. Aggressive bass will attack a peripheral bait, leaving more docile bass holding to the structure undisturbed. A fish on the outskirts of a tree often indicates that others dwell near similar branches.

Differing from a traditional linear fan cast, Tyler will fish both outside edges before moving toward the center. Once he has cast each side of the fan, Tyler begins moving inward toward the trunk. He probes junctions and crevices seeking to extract fish from those locations. He works toward the center of the tree and then places lures along the trunk from the deep end toward the shore.

If Tyler catches bass on one or more of those progressive casts, he draws the fish away from the structure, keeping the fight in the deep open water. As his casting numbers grow and the fish become more aware of his presence, Tyler may downsize baits and shift to finesse techniques. Ultimately, he aims at that optimally attractive ambush spot, adding that fish to the two or three others already in his live well.

Although his first skill was to master stumps, Tyler has become the king of laydowns. Similar saturation casting methods work for both. Those casts often yield multiple fish. The number of quality fish extracted from each structure distinguishes a next-level angler.

SWIM JIGS

When largemouth bass hit a swim jig, they "hit it to kill it." The aggression it prompts makes a swim jig one of the more exciting lures to fish. It is a noisy lure that displaces water when it moves.

Fishing a swim jig is an exercise in speed. The lure is retrieved as rapidly as the angler can crank. The basic technique is to reel in the jig quickly while keeping it slightly below the surface of the water. Keeping it submerged is crucial. Breaking the surface lowers the effectiveness of the lure. When fishing a swim jig, most anglers keep their rod tip in the 10 o'clock position instead of a more typical 12 o'clock slot. In that posture, the upward pressure on the lure comes from an angle.

While speed is the feature of the presentation, it does not have to be straight-line speed. Some anglers make sudden stops in their retrieve. This stop flares the skirt, changing the appearance of the bait. Another theory is that stops let the fish catch up to the lure.

Deflecting the lure is another way of amending the speed path. A typical use case for a swim jig would be to cast it near grass. Swim jigs are lures that can snag. As a result, they are seldom fished directly into cover. The jig would be retrieved so that it brushed against outward strands of grass, dragging on them. The intersection repositions the bait as it resumes its speed run.

Swim jigs provoke a reaction strike. Some anglers argue that a jig can look like a baitfish, but the lure itself looks little like a shad or a bream. It is hard to believe that bass would confuse this lure with any natural forage. A typical swim jig has a flattened or wedge-shaped metal jig head. The jig head is followed by a flared plastic skirt and a straight-shanked

Swim Jig with Grub Trailer. *Photo by Joe Kinnison.*

hook. Most, not all, anglers fish a swim jig with a trailer, and the most common trailer has a twist tail, either a curly tail worm or a grub. The trailer is most often hooked so that the tail curls downward. The curl deflects the lure during its quick retrieve.

Swim jigs are typically fished during calm conditions. The glassier the water, the better. Swim jigs do not have much flash, so these lures need to be seen and heard. Repeated casts are often necessary to entice swim jig bites. They work well with a fan casting technique.

While the lures have application all seasons, post-spawn is the most typical time to employ swim jigs. The lures are well suited to explore the periphery of mid-depth structures where bass recover post-spawn. Although spring is prime time, swim jigs can be used throughout the summer.

Specialized equipment improves the success rate with a swim jig. The lure is best fished with a bait casting reel, and that reel should have a fast gear ratio. Bait caster gear ratios generally vary between 5:1 and 9:1. A ratio of at least 7:1 is preferred for retrieving a swim jig. Fishing line also matters for a swim jig. The best line has minimal coil and minimal stretch. Next-level anglers use monofilament line for most swim jig presentations. Since the lure is generally fished on the edge of vegetation or in open water, light test is appropriate.

Some believe that the swim jig method was invented by accident. No matter how accomplished, every angler has poor casts from time to time. The natural reaction is to spin the crank on the reel and recover the lure as fast as possible. Elements of swim jig fishing resemble such hasty retrieves. Proper delivery of the bait looks a lot like an angler furiously reeling the lure back to the boat. It is not a bait that you "creep along," says Tyler.

The swim jig is Tyler's first-choice lure for big bass, and he has found a way to customize his bait so that it looks like nothing else in the water. Tyler Carriere is famous in bass fishing circles for his garage. The garage has been converted into a fishing man cave. Three walls are covered by a well-organized collection of poles and lures. He has a workbench covering the entire back wall. Lure customizations occur there.

In his garage, Tyler creates swim jigs that look like no other. He starts with a heavy jig head, ½ ounce or heavier, twice the weight of

Tyler Carriere's man cave. *Andy Crawford Photography. Used with permission.*

many commercial swim jigs. His preferred skirt color is a brown/green mix, but his swim jigs normally have a touch of flair. A few strands of orange or the occasional purple thread in the skirt give the jigs a distinctive look. Not only does he alter color schemes, Tyler changes the lengths of the skirts. Tyler trims the skirts short and flares them out. His experience is that less bulk presents a more attractive bite for the bass. A shorter skirt also causes more vibration.

The specialized swim jig is finished with a craw worm trailer. If you have never heard of a craw worm, you are not alone. As it sounds, it is a combination lure with the long thick torso of a worm and crawfish flappers at the end. The soft plastic piece produces lots of movement. The weight of the torso works like a traditional boot trailer, batting the lure up and down. Tyler calls it giving the jig some "thump." The flappers add action to those up and down deviations.

The weight of the jig head keeps Carriere's swim jig below the surface, the short skirt hides some of its mass while adding curiosity, and the craw worm gives it a floppy change of direction during the fast retrieve. Tyler adds action to the lure by bumping his rod to the left as he reels. This custom lure and unorthodox recovery piques the curiosity of many bass.

TOLEDO BEND RESERVOIR

The 185,000-acre reservoir on the border of Louisiana and Texas may qualify as a local lake for Tyler Carriere. For the rest of us, the lightning-bolt-shaped lake is remote and large. It has a whopping 1,200 miles of shoreline. Excluding the Great Lakes, Toledo Bend is the fifth largest lake in the United States.

Toledo Bend is so big that most places you look, you see water. Near the shoreline, the flat water is typically broken by fields of fractured tree stumps and the occasional living tree specimen. The surrounding topography is flat, making the shoreline post oaks a distinguishing feature of the area.

Toledo Bend was created in 1969 by flooding 65 miles of forest surrounding the Sabine River. A product of the method of its creation, Toledo Bend is so ridden with underwater hazards that parts of the lake are not safe for deeper hulled boats. As a partial solution to difficult navigation, a tree-free channel was cut the length of the lake, north to south. Submerged cover deteriorates over decades, but remnants of the original stumps at Toledo Bend survive 50 years later. Fishing such structures remains the order of the day.

With such extensive habitat within the lake, the challenge at Toledo Bend is to find which of the many structures hold fish. Those old stumps do indeed hold fish. The largest bass ever caught on Toledo Bend has been 15 pounds, three ounces. Reeling in 10-pounders is a fairly regular occurrence. Sporting ample habitat and big fish, Toledo Bend was rated the best bass fishing lake in the country in both 2015 and 2016.

Recently, the lake fell out of the Top 10 rankings. Lakes go through cycles, and Toledo Bend has cycled down in the last few years. Local guide Matt Loetshcer identifies flooding as the culprit. Toledo Bend Reservoir was out of its banks and above normal pool during substantial portions of 2018 and 2019. The flooding submerged grass beds for a long enough period to cause a dieback. Moreover, high water relocated the bass. The lake level has been stable in 2020, and fishing has returned to pre-flood prominence.

Toledo Bend is currently blessed with large schools of baitfish. Shad numbers are high, and bluegill are not far behind. Now back in their familiar habitat, the bass are gorging. Anglers have not quite caught on yet. The lake has been busy, but not pressured. To be competitive in tournaments in the reservoir, a five-bass stringer weighing in at 15 to 20 pounds has been necessary.

While the near-term outlook is improving, local fish and wildlife agents continue to work to return the lake to its former stature. Several bass have been fitted with radio transmitters. Their locations and activities are being tracked. The data will be used to improve habitats and regulations. Even with a reemergence program underway, big bass are catchable.

A lake of this size has habitat for every fishing style. Up lake, it has shallow and stained water. Down lake is deep and clear with depths nearing 110 feet. Tyler is a dirty water fisherman, sending him up lake during the spring and summer seasons. He puts in at the Cypress Bend boat launch, and he heads north under Pendleton Bridge.

On the water from the Cypress Bend launch, follow the channel north to the San Miguel arm for one of the best combinations of a navigable channel with deep ledges and extensive shallows. The water stays murky up this narrow arm. The northeastern shoreline could be described as craggy. It looks like someone spilled a bag of yard waste. The varied shoreline is protected by mudflats, some of which appear above water. Sediment from the flats keeps the water dark. Bass have lots of nooks and crannies from which to attack a passing swim jig.

The southeast side of the San Miguel arm is more developed. Pockets of piers exist on the rounded shoreline. Vegetation largely extends to the water's edge. Tyler suggests fishing shoreline bushes.

The farther an angler travels up the arm, the murkier the water becomes. Dark and less than a quarter mile across, the thin arm warms quickly in the spring. Back toward the main body of the lake, the mouth of San Miguel bay has some larger points. Bass congregate there before moving deeper during the heat.

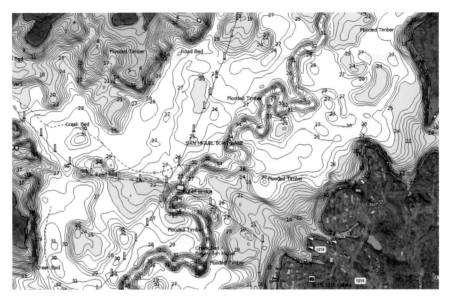

San Miguel Arm. Toledo Bend Reservoir. *Copyright 2021 Garmin Ltd or its subsidiaries. All rights reserved. Used with permission.*

Toledo Bend warms above 80 degrees Fahrenheit by June. At that temperature, bass seek cooler water with more oxygen content. Tyler suggests "drifting for days" along the river and creek channel ridges, picking up suspending bass. Regarding the main channel, Toledo Bend has an unusual fishing phenomenon. The hydropower plant near the dam runs periodically during the summer. It operates one to three hours at a time on a preannounced schedule. While the fish in most lakes get active when the water moves, the opposite seems to occur at Toledo Bend. Tyler believes that fish stop biting when the spillway opens. Thankfully, anglers can plan around the current.

Tyler recommends fishing down lake in the late summer and fall. He would look for fish on the deep edges of the flats. The lake continues to fish well into the holiday season.

Visitors traveling to Toledo Bend are going to experience the lake. The top of the lake is about 60 miles south of Shreveport, Louisiana.

It is reachable, but it is not close to any major city. The bottom of the lake is 70 miles north of Beaumont, Texas. The closest landmark to Toledo Bend is actually Sam Rayburn Reservoir, another top bass fishing locale.

Sam Rayburn is 25 miles west of Toledo Bend. However, the prime access point is south of the lake in Rayburn County. Add another 15 miles for that leg of the trip. The Tackle Addict is a legendary outfitter in that area, and The Stump is a popular restaurant for anglers. The longer drive to Sam Rayburn is worthwhile.

Neither lake is much fun in the wind. Both lakes are exposed, and both are filled with obstacles. As Toledo Bend is known for its timber, Sam Rayburn is known for its grasses. The Texas Department of Natural Resources keeps both lakes in top fishing condition. On calmer days, fishing enthusiasts might attempt the very different fishing styles required for each of these lakes.

Cypress Bend is the most fully featured access point to Toledo Bend Reservoir. The launch is accessible from Louisiana Highway 191. Cypress Bend park has a paved, six-lane boat launch, making it the largest entry point on the lake. It has the feel of being a superhighway (only everyone drives backward down the boat ramp). The parking lot at the boat launch holds 100 truck and trailer combinations. Although it has capacity for a crowd, Tyler warns that Cypress Bend can get extremely congested.

Near the ramp, Cypress Bend park has a pier, a pavilion, and a playground. Campsites are available from June through October. The park's best feature may be a large sand beach, which is a nice place to cool off on a Texas summer day. Boaters often anchor offshore from the beach or run their boats aground nearby.

While the hardcore anglers may head straight for the busy boat ramp, the nearby Cypress Bend Resort offers a broader array of recreational options. The resort is known for its grounds. It has large lawns and a number of gardens. The golf course is one of the few lakeside tracks in the area. At the main lodge, the resort has a swimming pool and a comfortable lobby. The three-star property is not luxurious but also not expensive. It houses one of the nicest restaurants in the area.

While perhaps not the nicest, the most memorable food in the area can be found about 10 miles east. Cars with boat trailers line up for miles to get a seat in the restaurant for breakfast. Toledo Town & Tackle serves Southern comfort food in overwhelming portions. The grits get especially high marks. It is the kind of place you would expect to see Guy Fieri and the *Diners, Drive-Ins, and Dives* crew.

Along with being a memorable food stop, Toledo Town & Tackle may be a necessary one. It is the only gas station for miles, and it also houses a fully assorted tackle shop. If you stop on your way to the lake, be sure to take a selfie at the four-foot high chrome bass statue.

For those intending to fish both major bass lakes in the region, steering west to the Texas side of the lake misses some attractions but saves some travel time. Convenient accommodations are available at the Midlake Campground. It has cabins and paved campsites among a grove of towering trees.

Due to the size of Toledo Bend and the hazards within, anglers new to the lake are advised to use a guide service. Some of the guides specializing in bass fishing are listed below.

Select Toledo Bend Fishing Guide Services

Gleason Fishing	337-397-8860	gleasonfishing@gmail.com
Joe Joslin Outdoors	337-463-3848	JoeJoslinOutdoors@yahoo.com
Living The Dream Guide Service	318-256-8991	ltdguideservice@gmail.com

GETTING STRUCTURED

For Tyler Carriere, the word "structure" means many things. Fishing physical structure, a stump or laydown, is his strength. Structure is also an organizing principle. Having a structured approach to fishing separates him from amateur anglers. Being orderly can make a meaningful difference in angling results.

A more systematic approach to fishing starts with a plan, which is then reassessed on a scheduled basis. Getting more structured starts off the water. Few anglers are unfailingly organized in their thoughts. Memory can be fleeting. To have data on which to base a fishing plan, prospective next-level anglers need to start writing. Make lists and write notes.

Tyler Carriere keeps journals in his boat, in his truck, and in his man cave. He records the essential facts of a fishing day, and he combines his notation time with devotional moments.

Keeping a fishing journal is a first step in elevating your angling. Over time, the notations accumulate to become powerful tactical information. Please see Appendix III for example fishing journal pages.

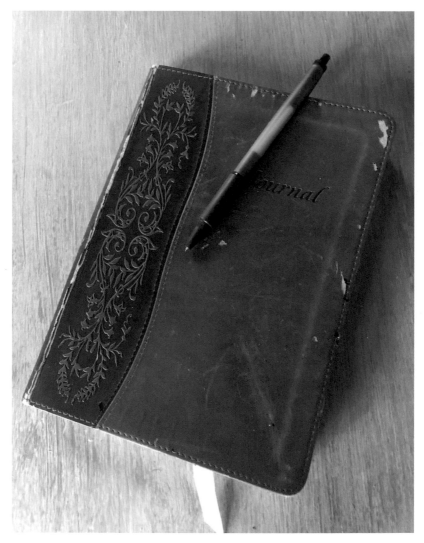

Fishing journal. *By Joe Kinnison.*

To begin a journaling discipline, start with standard environmental facts. Write down the conditions: air temperature, water temperature, wind direction and speed. After jotting down the situation, note for yourself which lures worked and which did not. If you were able to perceive a pattern, record that information as well. Highlight any learnings from your fishing day. Example insights include things such as "stop fishing the middle–depth cove in the fall" and "twitch crankbaits at least twice before starting the retrieve."

After assembling a fishing journal over many seasons, consult its contents prior to each new outing. Using your notes, formulate a plan based on expected conditions. For a 70-degree morning with overcast skies and light wind on a lake with bream forage may call for blue and chartreuse spinner baits to be fished on shallow flats. On previous fishing trips, you may have tried red squarebill crankbaits under similar conditions with limited success. You may have learned that baits started from the shoreline had more success than baits cast a few feet offshore.

With information from a journal, anglers can organize a fishing day. Make a schedule based on your data. Execute the plan with appropriate equipment and proper technique. Using the example above, one might start fan casting flats with blue or yellow lures. If that method proves successful, repeat it from flat to flat.

Having a written plan enables regular assessment. Some anglers tabulate bites, catches, and weights. Measurements open possibilities for analysis. If lures and locations are working, how well are they working? If your plan worked for a while and subsequently stopped, why did it stop? Conditions may change. The sun might come out. Activity levels on the water may change. Finding the fish once again is far easier once a deviation from a baseline can be detected.

Fishing journal data not only provides points of comparison, it can also be a tool to manage time. A danger of having a plan is getting married to it. If you predetermine to fish the shady side of structure in five feet of water and it does not produce bites, stop. Your original plan is not working. Instead of running out the clock by continuing to fish unproductive places, change. An hourly review of the effectiveness of your plan can make a fishing day much more productive.

Maintain a journal to add structure to your fishing day. It may raise your angling to the next level.

COMMUNITY

Away from the lakes and back home, Tyler Carriere's life has a different sort of structure, family structure. He lives in a subdivision home with his wife and children. The house is a few miles away from his parents' home. He is a devoted son and father. His grandmother no longer lives 185 miles north on the lake where the second-biggest bass in Louisiana formerly swam. However, he carries her memory close. Family is at the center of Tyler's fishing success.

Tyler, Carter, and Liam Carriere. *Photo by Carrie Carriere.*

When he is not towing his boat to a tournament, Tyler's boys can often be heard chattering in the back of his truck. He is a baseball dad most weekends. He is also passing on his fishing prowess when the kids are available. Carter Carriere and his partner Evan Hebert, Jr. finished fourth at a Toledo Bend Reservoir Jr. Bassmaster event last year.

Southern Louisiana is blessed with water. The Atchafalaya River is nearby, and five substantial ponds dot Tyler's subdivision. As a neighbor, it would be easy to be intimidated by a professional fisherman showing up at the neighborhood pond. Tyler's occasional presence does draw a crowd of onlookers and half-hearted challengers. On a typical visit, his youngest, Liam, will shuttle fish from the live well of his bass boat, down the chunky white riprap, to one of the ponds. With all of the Carriere deposits, these ponds must be teeming with bass.

Tyler cares for his family, his neighborhood, and the broader community. He promotes the local Shriners by wearing their logo on his fishing jersey. In addition, he uses lures from a friend's bait company whose manufacturing facility is nearby. Tyler's community has a champion on the professional fishing tour. Extracting multiple bass from each productive structure, he will be their representative for a long time to come.

CHAPTER 4
Technocrat:
A technical expert.[1]

Largemouth bass are, for the most part, a shallow-water species. They spend much of the spring and fall in as little as five feet of water, and they return from relative depths to the shallows on summer nights. Since the quarry is shallow, fishing electronics serve less purpose for bass anglers than for anglers of other fish species. Even today's best sonar modules are ineffective finding fish in shallow waters. As such, the utility of fishing electronics for bass anglers is in discovering structure that fish might frequent, as opposed to finding the fish themselves. In that sense, the instruments could rightly be called depth finders.

Although electronics are not optimal for finding shallow dwellers, they are useful in revealing depth changes and submerged cover. The contour of the bottom appears as a graph that runs right to left on most sonar systems. The graph will display slopes, bumps, indents, and ledges. In addition to topography, fishing electronics will display encumbrances. Fallen trees, standing stumps, and fish attractors appear in the scroll. Using down sonar, most of these structures appear as hairy triangular shapes rising from the bottom.

Most systems show bottom contours, and some devices recognize forage. Schools of baitfish can be visible as either scattered dots or as round masses moving in the mid-depths. Seeing these schools aids

---

1   Retrieved November 1, 2020, from https://www.merriam-webster.com/dictionary /technocrat.

largemouth bass anglers. Lunkers often locate themselves below group-
ings of baitfish.

ADJUSTMENTS

A few quick adjustments improve electronics for a largemouth bass angler.
Since the tool is not likely to identify fish in low single-digit depths, bass
anglers improve the utility of the device by reducing the surface clarity
setting to its lowest adjustment. Fishing electronics can register suspended
solids near the surface, and this data can cloud the shallow-water readout.
Minimize that feature. After adjusting down the surface noise, anglers
should next increase the sensitivity setting of the unit. Higher sensitivity
increases the likelihood of finding largemouth bass swimming in the shallows. Even though largemouth bass can occasionally exceed 15 pounds,
these are small fish relative to many other freshwater species, such as
northern pike, catfish, and spoonbill. Higher sensitivity settings increase
the odds of discovering and distinguishing a bass.

Adjustments made, some of the simplest features of sonar devices are
the most important to bass anglers. Many transducers sample water temperature, and water warmth is a key indicator for bass fishing. For example, a spring water temperature of 49 degrees implies a much lower level
of bass metabolism than a water temperature of 56 degrees. Knowing
the temperature may be sufficient to drive lure selection. Jerkbaits and
jigs would be effective in 49-degree water, whereas spinner baits and
crankbaits might get more bites at 56 degrees. Knowing the temperature guides retrieval speed, and charting temperatures in different areas
of a body of water will give an indication of where bass activity is likely
to be the highest. Bass are more likely to be feeding in 57-degree coves
than off 53-degree main lake points.

GPS is another common feature of onboard fishing electronics,
and it is a most useful application for bass anglers. With regular use of
electronics, next-level bass anglers can identify attractive underwater
structures and potential ambush points for the predator fish. Once discovered, stumps, brush piles, fish attractors, and ledges can be marked
as waypoints on most fish finders. Especially for those power fishing,

moving from waypoint to waypoint and knowing exactly where to cast can provide a significant advantage. Anglers use GPS coordinates to mark these fishing spots.

For those unimpressed with water temperature and GPS features, you may be even less excited about bottom hardness. However, the bottom density is a potentially deterministic feature for bass anglers. Fish tend to congregate along gravel bottoms and shell beds much more so than silted mud river and lake floors. Color displays indicate hard bottoms by displaying thinner returns for graphs mapping the bottom. Graphs often show a yellow lower boundary surrounded by red clutter. Thick yellow is a mushy lake floor where the odds of finding fish are low. A thin yellow stripe indicates hardness. As with down images, side-image sonars also indicate hard bottoms. Those images show a field of grit rather than traditional smooth surfaces. The grit looks something like aggregate finish on a concrete driveway. Using either thin down images or gritty side images, next-level anglers locate fish on hard bottoms.

THERMOCLINE

Like many of the other electronics features, for bass anglers, examination of the water column is not directed at the fish themselves. Instead, bass anglers focus on a temperature zone. Fish finders show when a thermocline sets up within a body of water during the summer months. A thermocline is a distinct layer that separates warm and cold water within a lake. Surface waters warm in July and August. As water temperatures meet or exceed 80 degrees, the aquatic environment becomes unfavorable for cold-blooded creatures. To further complicate matters, warm water fosters growth in plant life, and the resultant algae blooms can be harmful to fish. Those warm surface waters, called epilimnion by scientists, can be stirred by winds, boat props, and swimmers. Warm water is already more active chemically, and those outside forces further circulate the liquid. The circulation often leads to a higher level of dissolved oxygen in the water. More oxygen is generally a good thing for aquatic creatures. Those who have experienced a triple-digit summer day with humidity near

100 percent know that all you want to do is find somewhere shady with air movement where you could move as little as possible. That's what it is like to be a bass when the water temperatures rise to the '80s.

Lower in a lake, down 15 to 25 feet depending on water clarity, the situation is quite different. There, the water gets only filtered sunlight, currents are irregular, and swimmers are infrequent. These waters stay cooler, often year-round. Cooler water has higher density. The H_2O molecules move slower, have less vibration, and exhibit less energy. These waters have temperatures more accommodating to fish. Yet, comfortable temperatures come at a cost of lower dissolved oxygen. The human version of this experience would be visiting mountain elevations in the summertime. What you gain in cooler temperature, you lose in available oxygen. In these cases, the intensity of activity tilts downward.

The change in density between the warm, active upper layer and the cool, dense lower layer shows up on sonar. The thermocline marks the boundary between the warmer and cooler waters. On sonar devices, it shows up as a fairly straight echo keeping a constant depth as it is etched across the screen.

Waters near the thermocline have the best combination low temperature and high oxygen content available to bass during the dog days of summer. Largemouth bass continue to favor trees and brush piles where available. Absent those structures, they will gravitate toward steep underwater slopes. With the thermocline visible on fish finder display screens, anglers know to fish their lures at the depth where the thermocline layer intersects with either structure or slope. For example, if the thermocline is evident on sonar at 12 feet, a next-level angler will fish ledges at that same depth.

Thermocline layers tend to vanish in early fall. Cool evenings chill the previously warm upper layer, and the upper layer sinks. Once it sinks, the upper layer begins mixing with the lower strata. Something of a lava lamp situation ensues, with globs of water rising and sinking according to their temperature. This time is called the turnover period. It takes a few days for the water to normalize, and these are often among the worst fishing conditions of the year.

SIDE IMAGE AND 360

Side-image sonar is a feature on many newer electronic fishing aids. Side imaging adds perspective for the angler, but it can be difficult for an amateur to read. Different from down sonar, which shoots perpendicular to the surface, usually down in a 60-degree cone, side-image sonar shoots in parallel. Side image pings from a boat down to the bottom and then it extends at a 90-degree angle across the water body. Think of down imaging as an inverted V-shape. Think of side imaging as two "L's" connected at the shaft and facing opposite directions.

Less-expensive side-image systems default to 120-foot imaging. While that range is better than nothing, the spectrum is too wide for most largemouth bass anglers. At that span, bottom structure is evident, but fish themselves can be hard to find. For systems with an adjustment, a good rule of thumb is to change the side-image setting to current depth plus 30 feet. For example, an angler fishing in 10 feet of water would set the side-image sonar to span about 40 feet.

Whether using wide or narrow settings, laydowns, and brush piles proximate to the boat will be manifest as bright yellow shapes on the side-imaging readout. Structures directly below the boat will appear yellow in the black margins in the center of the screen. Outside of the center margins, side-image sonars display shadows below sonar contacts. Anglers can perceive distance from the bottom by observing the distance between the contact and its shadow. For example, a tree standing from the bottom will have a long shadow with the black relief of the top of the tree a long distance from the structure. A rock will have a shadow immediately behind the obstruction. Remember to look for grit if bottom hardness is present.

Anglers who can interpret the Rorschach chart will find bass with side imaging. Fish appear as white splotches among the yellow fields. Just like the structures, fish captured on side imaging also have shadows. The white splotches will have a matching black splotch slightly below them and in the same shape. These markings indicate that a fish is swimming a distance from the bottom.

Some fishing electronics manufacturers offer a 360-degree sonar option. These products require a special transducer that suspends below the bottom of a boat. 360-degree images look similar to side images, with the same color scale. The black margin is a circle in the middle of the screen, and the yellow fields extend in all directions around the boat, as opposed to either side of the craft. Being able to see topography emerging in front of the boat is a particular advantage of a 360 scan.

While making the general point that largemouth anglers tend not to use electronics specifically to find fish, that is not true in deeper bodies of water during the late summer. Thermocline notwithstanding, in midsummer and midwinter, largemouths will congregate on ledges in lake and river systems. In those cases, electronics are useful for their intended purpose, that being to identify fish. Down sonars will show inverted swoosh-looking characters to display suspended fish. With HD systems, anglers can see which way the fish are facing. This knowledge presents a significant advantage when deciding how to present a lure.

While the bass habitat defies some of the benefits of fishing electronics, temperature, GPS, and bottom hardness, information can elevate an angler. During summer months, knowing where the thermocline intersects the bottom is knowing where the fish are located. Next-level anglers need the ability to find fish on deep structure to be productive on clear sunny days and during heat waves. Skillfulness with fishing electronics differentiates anglers.

CHAPTER 5
Physiology:
A branch of biology that deals with the functions and activities of life.[1]

Flipping a tube bait to a narrow wedge of open air below a short, thick bush was the easy part. Brandon Palaniuk had emerged victorious from the ReelKids Casting Competition at Silver Lake Mall for two consecutive years. He could flip and pitch and cast a bass bug into one-foot-diameter rings as far away as 25 yards. The challenge posed by the shores of Hayden Lake was no greater. He raised his rod into the air, and he loosened the catch on the reel, allowing the tube to descend to the level of his hands. Once the lure reached proper position, he used his free hand to pull two arms lengths of additional line from his reel. From the reel out to his left hand and up to first eyelet on the rod, he had created a near-perfect triangle. The tube still hung freely a few inches away from his hand cradling the reel.

As he had done hundreds of times in his backyard, he raised and then lowered the tip of the rod aiming the pendulum of line and lure forward at his target. The tube swung along the apex of the line, and as it reached its full extent, he fed the triangle of drawn glass thread through the shrinking circular guides lashed to his rod. The tube lure angled under the bush and settled noiselessly into its shadow. He let out just enough slack to allow the lead bullet weight making demands on the line to draw the lure deeper.

---

1   Retrieved November 1, 2020, from https://www.merriam-webster.com/dictionary/physiology

Flipping technique. *By Will Frank.*

His fishing partner, Jeremy Tripp, was impressed by the execution of the flip. The twentysomething, backwoodsman-built family friend rubbed his short beard between his thumb and forefinger. He eased into his chair and patted the folds on his omnipresent blue jeans. He had expected to be a mentor for a green angler. Having seen the perfectly executed lure presentation, he decided to reassess.

Jeremy's surprise had something to do with his experience shoreside. Brandon had been awestruck at the first sight of the bass boat. The kid had traced the seams of the purple, green, and silver paint. It was flashy. It was awesome. He wanted to know everything he could about the maker, Skeeter. He marveled that such a large motor was fitted onto such a small boat.

Once Jeremy launched the boat at Cooper Bay marina, he showed Brandon what that big outboard could do. The front hull of the boat raised out of the water, and it raced several miles up the lake, leaving a plume of frothy water behind. Brandon did not give much attention to the pine stands steepening the relief of the Bitterroot Mountains on either side, nor to the rock-strewn shoreline. Likewise, he did not care that kokanee, landlocked sockeye salmon, was the primary fishing attraction of the lake. Brandon and Jeremy were on a powerful bass boat, and they would be fishing for bass. The boat slowed as it entered Mokins Bay, and it settled offshore from one of the few grassy banks.

Seconds after a carefully selected watermelon-and-black-flecked tube disappeared under the newly budding bush, Brandon's line started moving out from the tendrils of the plant and into the open water. Brandon snapped the rod tip upward and set the hook. The rod bowed as the bass surged toward the depths. Brandon kept tension on the line, and he played the fish expertly, finally hoisting the four-pound largemouth aboard. Beaming with self-satisfaction, he decided at that moment that he had discovered his vocation. Jeremy sensed it too. Different sorts of lessons were needed.

Jeremy and Brandon began entering fishing tournaments together, and for the next seven years, they fished competitions throughout the Northwest region. Over time, Jeremy counseled tournament strategy and the business of fishing.

Jeremy Tripp and Brandon Palaniuk. *Photo by Kyle Vandever.*

Armed with this knowledge, Brandon went solo upon turning 16 years old. He became the fishing version of a gym rat. He seemed to show up at every lakeside, and his only wardrobe appeared to be fishing togs. During tournament weekends, he would park his well-traveled Toyota Tundra near the boat launch and sleep in the front seat. He says he was saving money, but competitors suspect that he just wanted to be closer to the watershed.

Despite the fishing immersion, it took Brandon four years to rise to the top of the Western region. Having achieved regional recognition, he began another lengthy process to qualify for national events. He found his stride. Once he arrived on the national circuit, he made an instant splash. Brandon won the National Championship in his class in 2010. With his prize winnings, he bought a newer truck of the same model. For this one, he added a sleeper cab covering the truck's bed.

His first professional win came on the Red River in Louisiana; at least it was on the Red River for most tournament participants. Brandon had studied satellite imagery of the area, and he discovered a concealed and nearly inaccessible backwater pond. Based on the images of the bottom structure, he was certain that the pond held fish. Accessing it was another matter.

The plan was to break his boat through a dense berm of weeds separating the pond from the river. First, he tried to coast through the growth using his trolling motor. It lacked power to traverse the thicket. Taking the Tim "the Tool Man" Taylor "more power" approach,[2] at full throttle, the outboard motor nearly overheated. As a last resort, he leaned over the bow and hand-pulled his boat through the weedy berm and into open water in the pond. He accomplished the task, tugging one aquatic plant at a time. The buggy, muddy, snaky effort was worth it. His sense for locating fish was correct. He quickly filled his live well.

Since that day more than a decade ago, Brandon has not stopped fishing tournaments. As of this writing, he has appeared in 105 professional competitions in 10 years as a pro. He is fishing nearly every

---

2 *Home Improvement*. Performance by Tim Allen. 1991–1999.

Elite series tournament (eight are scheduled each year). Adding to his schedule, Brandon shows up at some regional tournaments and open competitions as well. To the great surprise of the occasional community bass club, he has been known to appear unannounced at a local tournament. The more he fishes, the more instinctual he feels on the water. That instinct is his advantage.

THE FISH WHISPERER

Brandon Palaniuk might be considered the fishing version of *The Horse Whisperer*.[3] In the 1998 movie, Robert Redford's Tom Booker character proves able to interpret subtle signals from the large animal. Through ear wiggles, snorts, eye movements, and gait changes, Booker is able to determine both the health of a stallion and its willingness to be trained. In the movie's signature moment, Booker lays the horse down on its side, sits atop the downed animal, and reacquaints a young equestrian with the beast.

Brandon is not one for cowboy hats, but he is seldom seen without a baseball cap. His often concealed, latte brown hair is cut shorter than his facial hair. Mirroring his concave eyebrows, a horseshoe mustache occasionally descends down from his frequently sunburnt nose. A young Redford was once described as having searching blue eyes. Brandon has that trait, although his comes with an intensity ground between his teeth. Like the Booker character, Brandon has incredible powers of observation. Both share a love for wildlife physiology, and both appreciate the animal to human interface. Brandon's animals just happen to live underwater.

Fish, like horses, have body language. Although ultimately getting a fish to bite is central to the sport, Brandon seems equally compelled by how a fish acts before capturing a lure. When retrieving a lure, he pays careful attention to the distance at which a fish follows a bait. He makes a mental note of whether it is closing distance or lagging behind

---

3   *The Horse Whisperer*. Directed by Robert Redford. Performances by Robert Redford and Kristin Scott Thomas. 1998. https://www.imdb.com/title/tt0119314/.

the retrieve. If he can see the fish, either visually or on electronics, he tracks whether the animal is below the bait, above the bait, or in the same level of the water column. He samples the responses to changes in speed and direction.

Once a bass bites, another information deluge begins. In what part of the mouth is the fish hooked? How aggressive was the bite? How vigorous was the fight? Brandon gets a good sense of the attitude of the fish.

The sensory load continues once the fish reaches the boat. When he can see more of the bass, Brandon records its shading. According to a Department of Energy study, largemouth bass can change the shade of their skin by alternately expressing or masking green and brown pigments.[4] Black spots along the lateral line may also darken or lighten. This color change is believed to be caused by hormones, and it is a natural camouflage mechanism. Bass tend to express more white tones when they reside in deeper water. While more white shading may be counterintuitive, less distinct markings make the fish harder to see in darker water, especially when viewed from below. Bass exhibit more green tones when they suspend in clear water and near the surface. An angler who is observant to coloration can have insight into the water level from which the fish came.

Along with skin pigment, Brandon appreciates the eyes as well. Bass have photosensitive cells in their eyes. Like the skin, eye pigments can be altered. The pigments can change from white to black to adjust their permeability to available light. This works much in the same way as human pupils widen in low light and narrow in bright light. A wider pupil would look black to an observer. In a similar way, the dark adjusted structures in a fish's eyes will look black. To an angler, the eyes of the fish can give clues to the depth and water clarity.

While coloring can key location and aggressiveness, Brandon looks to the fins for additional data. The tail, scientifically the caudal fin, is the power source for bass. With this fin, the species can swim at speeds exceeding 12 miles per hour. The caudal fin will redden

---

4 Hanson, Debbie. "What colo is your largemouth bass?" Takemefishing.org. 2/3/14.

seasonally when the fish are post-spawn. Markings can reveal the spawning stage.

Although the caudal fin can clue spring pattern, the pectoral fins can provide the most regular information to an angler. The fins mostly serve to control change of direction. Pectoral fins are positioned on the sides of a bass's body positioned immediately behind the gill slits. Pectoral fins are spiny with 14 to 16 ribs within each one, and they work independently. One fin flared and the other flat helps turn the fish. Both fins flared may act as a brake. The fins can be flapped for a momentary boost in speed. To the angler, flattened pectoral fins indicate a more linear fight, and spread pectoral fins indicate attempts at maneuvering. By examining the fins, Brandon can determine how a bass might be approaching its prey.

Anglers, especially professional ones, prefer to target large fish. "Big fish are different," reports Brandon. Big bass tend to hold tight to underwater structures, touching them in many cases. The location of their territories may depend on climate control. Brandon believes that big fish are more temperature sensitive than small fish. Fish five pounds and larger show a strong preference for cooler water. As such, catching a larger bass may indicate the depth of the temperate water.

While big fish are the target, anglers often reel in small ones. The size of each fish reeled in offers interesting details about the fish as well. The length of a bass generally tells its age, with bass exceeding a foot in length in their fourth year in most seasonal states. Younger bass generally school, so catching a small bass likely indicates the presence of other similarly sized fish.

Brandon does not admit to whispering to the fish. Yet, by the time he reads their body language, he may know all that he needs to know. In the event he misses a signal, he consults his videographer aboard to film every catch.

SWIM BAITS

It may not be a surprise that a "fish whisperer" wants his lure presentations to be natural. His favored lures resemble baitfish in color, size, and action. Swim baits offer the most lifelike solutions.

As a native of Idaho, Brandon has a claim to the lure that achieved national prominence after notable catches in West Coast reservoirs. Swim baits have existed for decades. However, the lifelike lures became popular in the 1990s when they started catching record-setting bass in the western lakes. Swim baits entered into the national fishing consciousness after they were used to win a 2007 Bassmaster Elite tournament.

Along with high water clarity favoring the greater realism of swim baits, presentation of the lure draws upon techniques familiar to trout anglers who are more prominent in the mountain regions. As with trout fishing, in fishing swim baits, small details matter. Anglers have lost wary fish to aspects as minute as the length of their shadow or the color of their garment. With these sorts of flaws to contend with, the more lifelike the lure, the better.

Swim baits have a reputation for attracting big fish, but they also have a reputation for attracting relatively few bites. As with most lures, speed and depth of retrieve are the keys. Swim baits are often reserved for deep water. They have been fished successfully down beyond 50 feet. Viewed as a deepwater bait, swim baits are fished seasonally post-spawn through the summer.

Several styles of swim bait exist—soft, hollow, and hard. Soft swim baits are the least natural-looking. They are formed from plastic. The body of the lure has ridges and valleys much like the treads on a tap bolt. Think of that bolt with a line tied to the threads and the head trailing behind. Where the bolt head would be, a swim bait has a foot, made to mimic a fish's caudal fin. The flopping foot gives a swim bait some swish in the water. Occasionally fished with a solitary hook, soft swim baits are most often hooked to a jig head. Umbrella rigs are frequently populated with soft swim baits.

More realistic than soft swim baits, hollow swim baits are plastic molds made to look like a minnow. Most have an opening near the minnow's mouth, and another opening anterior to where pelvic fins would be on a real fish. Fishing line is fed from the rod and through the mouth. It ties to a treble hook below the rear opening of the bait. The hollow frame wrinkles when retrieved, looking like real skin.

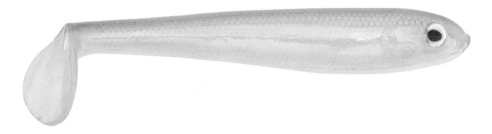

Shadalicious Sexy Swim Bait Blue Back Herring. *Courtesy of Strike King.*

Hard swim baits are made of firm plastic pieces fastened together with metal swivels. Hard swim baits usually have two or more joints. These versions of a swim bait look most like the fish they mimic. The movements of the bait at the joints provide a pretty convincing avatar of a fish swimming.

The choice of soft, hollow, or hard swim bait often depends on the Rate of Fall (ROF) desired from the bait. Before accounting for added weights, hard swim baits are the heaviest. As such, they have the fastest ROF. Hollow swim baits tend to be the lightest and most buoyant. They descend slowly through the water.

The typical presentation of a swim bait is to start the retrieve below the level at which the fish are believed to be suspending. To begin, let the lure fall at its designed rate from the surface to below the depth where the bass are holding. For example, if sonar images show bass suspending at 15 feet, the swim bait would be allowed to descend to about 18 feet prior to the start of the retrieve. Be aware that bass may bite the lure on the fall.

Although sinking the lure to just below suspending bass is the traditional approach, other options can lead to bites. While it is not a first-choice method, dropping a swim bait all the way to the bottom can be a successful technique, especially in the winter season. Bass can confuse a bottoming swim bait for a dying baitfish. Shad in many lakes die off in the early winter.

Assuming it is not winter, let's return to plan A. Once at the desired depth, swim baits work most effectively when fished using an uphill retrieve. An uphill retrieve simply moves the lure from deep water to shallow water. This deep to shallow migration can be performed regardless of ultimate water depth. While fishing uphill, swim baits work best when dwell time in a bass's strike zone is maximized. To make the most of time in the strike zone, the uphill retrieve need not be linear. An angler can drop her rod tip and keep the swim bait at a constant depth for a few additional seconds. Alternatively, the bait can be drawn higher and the reeling then paused to drop the lure back into the strike zone. A general movement uphill while maximizing time in the strike zone is the right idea.

With the ideal situation being a long, steady, uphill retrieve, not every terrain is suitable for the bait. Ledges, bluff walls, and the sides of points are good swim bait locations. Near such structures, the baits can be fished to stay the strike zone for long portions of each cast. Swim baits are seldom fished to make contact with structure. They are not reaction lures. The angler is not trying to deflect off an underwater object or speed past an aggressive fish. To the extent they are fished near cover, the lures are generally fished parallel to grasses, timber, and riprap. Exposed hooks on hollow and hard varieties make the lures subject to snags. The lures rely on their realistic appearance to draw fish away from suspension or out of slope-side cover.

Swim baits are often fished slowly. However, slowly does not mean lifelessly. Brandon believes in providing action for these lures. He animates the bait so that it takes on the appearance of an actual fish. He twitches it to make it wiggle. He alters the direction of his rod tip from three o'clock to nine o'clock to change the direction of travel. He makes short pauses to create a suspending moment, and then as the line recovers, a darting action. Altering the bait's constructed movement pattern to create something lifelike is the aim.

Brandon prefers to create an even more erratic action once he sees a trailing fish. Bass frequently follow the swim baits for some distance before biting. One mistake that new anglers often make is to stop the bait once they see a fish in pursuit. Stopping the forward motion gives the bass an opportunity to study the lure. To prevent the examination, he will speed up his reeling or make a sudden change of direction.

Brandon's signature move is a spin-move. A basketball player performs this maneuver to escape a defender. Brandon spins his lure to trigger a trailing fish. Sometimes, he is able to spin the lure to face its pursuer. He starts by tightening the line and pointing the tip of the rod down near the water level. Next, he will jerk the rod to one side. Finally, he will raise it high and forward toward the fish. This series of movements will turn the lure toward the onrushing bass. All of these efforts—change speed, change direction, and spin—are all designed to force the beast to make a quick decision.

Brandon's first swim bait cast will generally present a glide bait. A glide bait is a large, hard swim bait with more aggressive movement characteristics. Depending on the level of response, he will often make subsequent casts with smaller soft versions. If a few casts do not produce a bite, Brandon moves to different underwater terrain. Swim baits are finesse presentations, and he sees no purpose in pounding an unproductive area with dozens of casts.

Swim baits are heavy lures, and they work best with heavy tackle. Seven-foot rods are recommended, and those should have a heavy

Brandon Palaniuk casting a swim bait. *Selfie.*

backbone and allow for parabolic bend. Fluorocarbon fishing line is the least visible type of line, and it should be employed for these clear-water lure presentations. Brandon recommends a 20-pound test. Bait casting reels with low gear ratios and large crank handles are optimal for the big, slow-moving swim baits.

The proper attitude is as important as the proper gear for swim bait fishing. Anglers would be best served to approach throwing this bait with the intention to attract the bite of a single large fish. Swim baits are not an appropriate choice for anglers looking for lots of action.

LAKE COEUR D'ALENE

Brandon's favorite lake is one close to home. Lake Coeur D'Alene is a natural glacial lake now dammed for water management purposes. The lake is 30 miles west of Spokane, Washington, and it fills mountain valleys south of the city of Coeur D'Alene, Idaho. Coeur D'Alene is a top-10 bass fishery in the West and a top-50 fishery in the United States. The lake holds Idaho state records for both freshwater Chinook salmon and cutthroat trout. Lake Coeur D'Alene is a popular locale for anglers of northern pike. Pike larger than 20 pounds are considered trophy size, and fish of that size and larger are caught regularly.

Lake Coeur D'Alene has a reputation for cold water. The lake is northern, and it is situated at relatively high altitude, above 2,000 feet. Latitude and altitude marshal the heat. Parts of the lake freeze over in the winter. Lake temperatures stay in the 50s into the month of June before peaking in the low 70s in August. For largemouth bass, whose happy place is the 60- to 70-degree zone, that window of optimal conditions is late and short.

What it lacks in temperature, Coeur D'Alene more than makes up for in terrain. The maple-leaf-shaped lake is fed by two rivers. The St. Joe River flows into the headwaters of the lake, and the Coeur D'Alene River feeds a chain of lakes before spilling into the reservoir mid-lake. The rivers provide current and smaller, warmer habitats for the fish. Largemouth bass are most prevalent on the south end of the lake, which is shallower and closer to the river inflows.

For a prominent lake, fishing records are sparse. Official records only date to 2016. The biggest largemouth caught since then is 9.7 pounds. Official statistics aside, most agree that the biggest largemouth bass ever caught in the lake was 10.9 pounds. These fish are lunkers given the climate. Local anglers know the lake's promise. The lake hosts a half dozen prominent bass tournaments per year. Winning five-fish stringers average in the low-to-mid-20-pound range. The population of four- to five-pound bass must be extensive.

Most visiting largemouth anglers access the lake from Harrison, a summer hamlet of 200 residents located 15 miles south of the dam. Highway 97 is the main artery. Harrison has a large marina on the lake-side edge of the Coeur D'Alene River terminus.

The Gateway marina is framed by weathered wood planking that makes you feel like you need to wear shoes. The boat slips sit protected by a mounded rock breakwater. In the summer, it is a rollicking dock-age full of speedboats, houseboats, personal watercraft, water adventure excursion boats, and the occasional float plane. Departing Harrison on a bass boat feels like going fishing in a resort area.

Off the dock, the hub of activity in Harrison is a trading post. The store is an adequate outfitter, but it is mostly for the hard candy stick crowd. The trading post serves deli-style sack lunches provisioning the crowd of day adventurers. Elsewhere for food, One Shot Charlie's is a destination tavern with a varied menu. Grinders get the accolades among the food choices. One Shot Charlie's has a sunset-facing deck and regular live entertainment.

Part of the resort feel comes from the presence of other outdoor pursuits. Harrison is not only a launching point for anglers, it is a destination for cyclists. The town itself is an outpost on the 73-mile scenic bicycle ride, the Trail of the Coeur D'Alenes. The Harrison to Chatcolet Bridge segment of the trail is the most popular spur for day riders and families. The Chatcolet Bridge is a marker for bass anglers too.

Along with anglers and cyclists, birders frequent Harrison. The Thompson Lake Wildlife Refuge occupies 1,000 acres north of town. Birders tour the refuge to catch glimpses of rare raptors. Peak migratory patterns occur in early May. Visiting anglers begin to outnumber birders during June.

Tourists and anglers with a week to stay head to the Red Horse Mountain Ranch. The dude ranch is a fully featured, all-inclusive resort south of town. Some weeks are reserved for adults and some weeks are family-oriented. Plan accordingly. Harrison has few options for overnight accommodations. Travelers on a one- to two-day time-line often find space at the Lakeview Lodge, and there are B&Bs in town.

While the cyclists and birders fill the town, most largemouth bass anglers leave the marina and either head upriver into a chain of lakes or they motor seven miles uplake. That route crosses under a Chatcolet Bridge spanning the old river channel. Chatcolet and Round Lake are prominent sections of the larger lake. The south end of Lake Coeur D'Alene has shallow water in relation to the main lake. Maximum depths near 35 feet, compared to 200-foot depths down lake. Several bays have large flats with single-digit depths. If the fish are not on the flats, two significant points, one above water and one hidden, will likely hold fish.

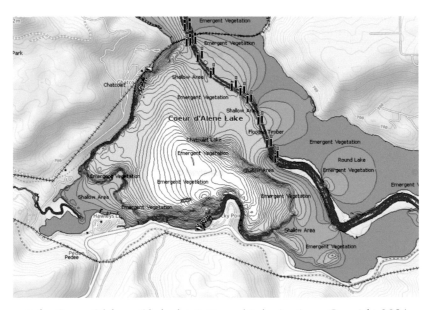

Lake Coeur D'alene. Chalcolet & Round Lake Sections. *Copyright 2021 Garmin Ltd or its subsidiaries. All rights reserved. Used with permission.*

Rocky Point is a landmark on this end of the lake. The land juts out like a hitchhiking thumb, making a peninsula several hundred yards long. The point has heavy tree cover, and a few docks extend from the thumbnail area. Offshore, the point has steep banks on all three sides, dropping from five feet deep to more than 20. Bass will stack up on the submerged slopes.

The hidden point is offshore from Heyburn State Park. A remnant of the St. Joe River flows into the lake in this area. With the normally clear water, the river channel can be observed from the surface, even several hundred yards offshore. The channel has mounds on either side. The eastern side is studded with rock formations, some of which emerge from the water. The point is made of this collection of features. Through the water, it looks like black sea glass, and it keeps a pretty steady 10-foot depth starting from the inlet. It eventually drops off to 30 feet on the exposed sides. Bass can be attracted to both the inlet and the ledges.

Bass move selectively in cool water, so successful anglers often employ slower moving lures. Jigs and soft plastic worms on drop shot riggings are successful presentations according to many fishing reports. Rock-laden points seem to hold fish, and people frequently get bites on the lakeside edge of grass beds. Brandon's swim baits seem well suited to the latter.

Largemouth bass anglers tend to fish the area from Harrison south. The northern end of Lake Coeur D'Alene has habitat more suitable for smallmouth bass. Different from the shallow-dwelling largemouth, smallmouth bass prefer to suspend far offshore. In most parts of the country, this species of bass migrates seasonally from 10-foot depths to 30-foot depths. In lake Coeur D'Alene, they go deeper. Much deeper. Anglers may have to make heavy use of fishing electronics to find smallmouth.

Like their largemouth cousins, "smallies" like structure. Their preferred habitat is a rockpile or a reef, and they will congregate on offshore humps. The north end of the lake has half a dozen humps that drop from 30 feet down to 90 or more.

While relating to structure, smallmouth bass do not make contact with rocks, stumps, and humps as a largemouth bass would. Smallmouth bass suspend a few feet above the bottom. Given their location, smallmouth are best caught with drop shot rigs or by jigging. Additional popular lures for smallmouth bass are spoons and tubes. Anglers jigging these lures would drop them to the sides of the hump and raise the rod tip to pull the lure up into the smallmouth strike zone.

Smallmouth bass are fighters. Hooked fish dive deep or surge toward open water. Anglers employing light gear are more apt to land the fish if they allow several minutes to raise the fish up to the boat. With differences in location, gear, lures, and techniques, anglers on Coeur D'Alene will pursue either largemouth or smallmouth bass. One of the recommended guides, Fins & Feathers, only targets the smallmouth species.

Select Coeur D'Alene Fishing Guide Services

Fins & Feathers	208-667-9304	finscda@frontier.com
Premier Charters	208-599-0409	vicki@premier-charters.com
Row Adventures	866-836-9340	ac@rowadventures.com

BIOLOGY

Brandon Palaniuk's deep understanding of fish physiology elevates his fishing. For an amateur angler trying to ascend to the next level, appreciating the physical attributes of their quarry provides a good starting point.

Many human anatomy teachers initiate their students by orienting them to parts of the body. Students learn the Latin terms for nearly every muscle, nerve, and joint. Instead of locating the lobulus auriculae and integumentum as they would with a human, anglers would begin to understand fish anatomy by finding features such as opercles and nares.

For both biology students and anglers, anatomical terms can be difficult to read and retain. Pronouncing the names aloud is a recommended practice to help ultimate recall. You may think it sounds silly to voice these words, but the exercise does work. Start by saying "opercle" three times aloud.

Classifying fish anatomy is a beginning. However, acing anatomy to the point of documenting the ribs on a pectoral fin will not fill your live well. Gaining a conception of the function of the anatomical parts does matter. Fish have systems. Different organs work together to provide respiration, propulsion, camouflage, and other essential processes. Respiration, for example, engages multiple organs, including the mouth, the gills, and the opercles.

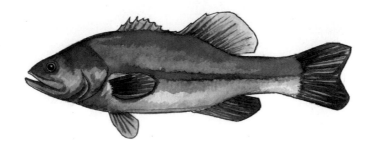

Bass physiology. *By Will Frank.*

Understanding systems can provide an angler clues to fish activities. Feeding is the function about which anglers are most interested and often engages as many as three anatomical systems. To consume a bait, bass must see the lure, feel its vibrations, and not be cautioned by its taste. For a fish to bite, the eyes, the lateral line, and taste receptors must be engaged.

First, consider sight. An angler benefits by knowing that a bass can see no more than 50 feet to either side. They also would be more efficient in realizing that the fish see nothing below or behind them. Lures should be presented relatively close to the animal, in front and above the level at which it is swimming.

Importantly, bass have a focal point five to 12 inches in front of their snout. As mentioned earlier, bass vary their distance behind swim baits to try to get a clear view in their forward field of vision. Next-level anglers know to prevent the fish from getting into critical range to get an optimal look at a lure.

Along with manipulating a bait in a bass's field of vision, under-standing how bass taste prospective food is essential to good fishing. Fish do not necessarily taste with their tongue. Instead, fish have taste receptors at several places on their skin. The taste receptors are located on the gill covers and on the peduncle, a muscle near the tail. Bass bump into baits to discern salty, bitter, or sweet sensations. Anglers briefed in fish physiology know how to adjust when they are getting bumps but not bites.

RAISING HIS VOICE

Brandon's ability to make his lure presentations ultrarealistic earns him a few extra bites each fishing day. Using physiology, he has become one of the leading money winners on the Bassmaster Elite tour. No longer entirely a whisperer, Brandon's voice now inflects. He is excitable and authoritative.

Each fish that he brings aboard is admired. He repeats "Oh my gosh," in a breathlessness that increases according to the size of the bass. From clipped exclamations, he transitions easily to being a spokes-man for finesse fishing techniques. The mix of marvel and media savvy sounds like one of the instant sideline reports following an important play in the brief return of the XFL football league.

CHAPTER 6
Wellness:
The quality or state of being in good health especially as an actively sought goal.[1]

HEALTH

Next-level anglers are athletes. While other sports train by running or weightlifting, getting into fishing shape has other requirements. Endurance may be the biggest fitness aspect for anglers. Core strength is a close second.

Professional tournament participants experience two consecutive practice days where they fish from sunup to sundown. They are standing and casting most of that time. Days get only slightly shorter during the four ensuing tournament days. Anglers fish for eight to nine hours. Few other sports have up to six consecutive days and more than 50 hours of competitive activity.

Standing on a moving bow for long hours builds back and hip muscles. In that way, resisting the roll of the waves builds core strength. Fishing builds muscle tone in similar fashion to some yoga postures. While promoting core strength, fishing also helps balance. An angler makes compensations for the moving hull. Over time, those sea legs bolster leveling. Along with balance, fishing exercises the shoulders and arms. A tournament angler can make 3,000 casts during an event.

---

1   Retrieved November 1, 2020, from https://www.merriam-webster.com/dictionary/wellness

An active pursuit that promotes core strength, fishing burns calories, about 200 per hour. While fishing is not aerobic exercise, a day of fishing requires more than 1,500 calories above the amount a person normally consumes in a day. At that rate of energy burn, hydration and nutrition merit attention for anglers who fish over long periods of time. Next-level anglers take regular hydration breaks and make high-energy food choices. Preparing to withstand the rigors of competitive fishing certainly is a positive for one's health.

The health benefits from fishing are not limited to the physical. Aspects of fishing are meditative. Anglers can focus their minds on a particular object, like the spot where a fishing line enters the water. Heightened attention and increased awareness can promote tranquility and mental health.

ACCLIMATIZATION

Fishing is, of course, an outdoor sport. Benefits accrue to anglers spending time in the elements. Vitamin absorption and acclimatization are among the perks.

While excessive sun exposure can be negative, limited time in the sunlight has positives. Next-level anglers are cognizant of the potential for sunburn, and most apply lotions and wear protective clothing. Some even wear face shields and gloves. With proper sun protection applied, human skin absorbs some UVB rays. These rays trigger the body to manufacture vitamin D. Vitamin D is stored in the body, and it is utilized as needed to make a chemical called calcitriol. Calcitriol helps the body absorb calcium, and calcium helps bone strength and cell function. About 15 micrograms of vitamin D per day is widely believed to boost one's immunity to disease.[2] Daily intake of up to 100 micrograms stays within the optimal range. Frequent anglers tend toward the high end of the range. This exposure is differentiating. Over 42 percent of the

---

2   Bjanrndottir, Adda. "How much vitamin D should you take for optimal health?" *Healthline*. June 4, 2017.

US population is believed to be vitamin D deficient. Few among this group are likely to be anglers.

Anglers are accustomed to being out in the weather, and human bodies adjust to their climate over time. For example, Minnesotans go to the swimming pool when it's 75 degrees out because it feels relatively warm to them. That same 75 degrees feels cold to a Floridian in summertime. Bodies adjust to their climate, but some bodies adjust faster than others. The speed of adjustment to heat or cold is called thermoregulation. Anglers with time spent outdoors thermoregulate more quickly than most people.

Acclimatization can prevent disease states. Raynaud's disease is an affliction in which people adjust slowly to cold. People with this affliction can require medical attention and even suffer frostbite when temperatures drop suddenly. Extreme heat has its own challenges. Pam Martin-Wells says, "100 degrees is just different," referring to one's ability to function under climate challenges. To handle heat and humidity, anglers have some cultural practices. Many minimize exposure to air-conditioning while preparing for hot-weather tournaments. Others conduct preparatory workouts scheduling them for the midday heat. Even with advance work, tournament anglers hydrate and drape cold towels around their necks. Spending more time outside than most, anglers are more prepared to accommodate temperature changes and more adaptive to them as they occur.

Along with a boost to immunity and some environmental seasoning, anglers benefit from connecting with nature. A 2016 paper from Miles Richardson concluded that exposure to nature improves "vitality, creativity, happiness, pro-social behaviour and pro-environmental behaviour."[3] At the core, humans connect to the natural world. Despite our efforts to control temperature, shut out bugs, and the like, most people have an inclination toward fresh air, flowers, and clean water. Anglers take it a step further by trying to understand aspects of the

---

3   Richardson, Miles. "Nature: a new paradigm for well-being and ergonomics." *Pubmed.gov*. March 22, 2016. https://pubmed.ncbi.nlm.nih.gov/26910099/.

natural world. For example, most successful anglers can immediately tell you the water temperature, wind speed, and the type of bugs that are hatching. Connections to nature lift the human spirit.

SUPPORT SYSTEM

Fishing is seldom a solitary sport. Statistics indicate that most anglers fish with a partner. Tournaments are organized to combine front-of-the-boat with back-of-the-boat participants. Even professionals seldom leave the dock without an accompaniment, like a driver, coach, photographer, or videographer.

Support systems for bass anglers are necessary both on and off the water. Families enable the activities of most next-level anglers. Some help with their presence. Some help with their absence from fishing venues. Tournament fishing requires heavy travel. Touring families provide meals, laundry, and moral support to anglers. While company and creature comfort works for some anglers, others find family responsibilities on competition days to detract from their fishing effectiveness. Tyler Carriere resumed fishing upon prompting from his wife, and his children often shadow him on tour. Whatever the most comfortable family arrangement, familial harmony plays a part in next-level fishing success.

Just as family support promotes fishing success, friends broaden one's knowledge base and provide trusted advisers. Fishing friends have confidence lures that likely differ from yours. One may trust chartreuse crank baits, while another may rely on june bug–colored trick worms. Different tactics work in different situations, and sometimes "seeing what is working" proceeds better with two people experimenting. Friends can also be advisers in sharing trusted information on lake conditions and fishing spots. Friends almost always provide perspective. A funny or an inspirational meme before takeoff can ease competitive pressure.

Few anglers reach the next level without a support system comprised of family and friends. Aid may range from personal services to confidence-boosting guidance. Velma Kelly, the character in the musical

Chicago, has the right idea when she chants the song "I Can't Do it Alone."

ECONOMICS

Despite all of its positive attributes and broad supports, a bass fishing lifestyle can be a difficult one. Equipment is expensive. A low-end bass boat costs $50,000. A more typically outfitted unit prices out in the $80,000 range.

Tournament fees can be steep. Bassmaster Elite entry fees amount to $5,375 per angler per tournament. FLW events cost $1,700 each. Phoenix Bass Fishing League offers a more affordable entry point at $200.

Registration fees are only half the battle. Anglers must pay for travel to fishing venues. Several-hundred-mile drives are common. For example, 1,200 miles separated two Bassmaster Elite tour stops in 2020. Using IRS reimbursement rates, transportation costs would have been near $700 for that trip.

Costs do not end with one's arrival at the tournament venue. With two to three practice days and two to four tournament days, a hotel or campground stay could be as long as seven days. Lodging costs likely exceed transportation expenses.

Costs are high, and they may not be covered by tournament prizes. Last year, the Bassmaster Elite average prize money per angler per tournament was $7,500. At those levels, net winnings after entry fees, travel, and equipment maintenance are negligible.

Averages do not tell the whole story. Payoffs are uncertain in general and low in aggregate. In a typical national tournament, anglers must finish in the top 50 merely to recover their entry fee.

Professional tournament winners do have a big payday. Bassmaster Elite top prizes ranged from $100,000 to $120,000 in the most recent season. FLW winners took home $40,000 for winning a tournament.

Tournament wins are by no means a given. Several Bassmaster Anglers of the Year have won the championship tournament without a top finish during the season. Multiple wins in a fishing season are extremely rare (albeit Brandon Palaniuk accomplished the feat in 2020). FLW has an award for the winner of their season series. It is $200,000.

Among the best of the best bass anglers fishing the national tours, only 10 percent earn more than poverty-level income from tournament prizes. Recent figures put the level just above $17,000 for a family of two.

Given the financial hurdles, it is not surprising that anglers get creative in their financial lives. Brandon Palaniuk achieved some level of renown for sleeping in his truck during several seasons' worth of tournaments. Although he received the most attention for the practice, he says that he is not the only angler that lives this way. Pinching pennies is something of a necessity for those trying to make a living by fishing.

Along with cost cutting, most professional anglers have a second job. Destin DeMarion and Tyler Carriere are fishing guides; Christiana Bradley works in IT; Pam Martin-Wells teaches college.

Financial stress is a real and often present issue for many anglers. Those who can overcome these pressures are at a distinct advantage. Sponsorships offer opportunities to defray a portion of the cost. Many sponsors provide complimentary gear, and some write checks. Committed sponsors improve the economic picture for competitive anglers.

Next-level fishing improves health and aids acclimatization, but it requires a strong support system and a level of economic sacrifice. Passionate anglers see more positives than negatives in the trade-off.

CHAPTER 7
Acuity:
Keenness of perception.[1]

Strong sensory perception is a trait that most accomplished anglers possess. Brandon Palaniuk sees details as minuscule as ribs on the fins of a fish. Pam Martin-Wells is acutely attuned to sound. To some extent, these gifts are God-given. However, for anglers less blessed, sense impressions can be heightened through conditioning.

In 2014 the University of California, Riverside, baseball team submitted to visual acuity training.[2] The players spent 25 minutes per day on exercises to improve spatial perception and peripheral vision. After several months of participation in the protocol, the positive changes in their sight were dramatic. On average, players increased their ability to see details, like lettering on a baseball, from a distance of 7.5 feet to more than 20 feet. Peripheral vision expanded by 31 percent. The sensory enhancement produced measurable higher batting averages.

Like baseball players, good anglers utilize several visual tools. Depth perception is an essential for effective casting. Perceiving light saturation helps identify underwater targets. Peripheral vision is crucial for picking up movement.

If sensory training works for baseball players, can anglers achieve similar benefits? Absolutely. Sense acuity may be the single most

---

1 Retrieved November 1, 2020, from https://www.merriam-webster.com/dictionary /acuity
2 Deveau, Jenni et. al. "Improved vision and on-field performance in baseball through perceptual learning." *Current Biology*. 2/14/2014. https://www.cell.com/current -biology/fulltext/S0960-9822(14)00005-0.

important personal quality for an angler. However tuned your senses, acuity training can make them better.

THINGS TO AVOID

To a degree, potent senses come from avoiding modern obstacles. Most people have heard that staring at screens is bad for you. It is true that long periods of screen time damage a person's eyesight. More than 50 percent of regular computer users show symptoms of eyestrain. A specific medical diagnosis has been created for more serious maladies. Computer vision syndrome is a repetitive-motion injury that is caused by constraining a person's field of vision to a small area. To the benefit of their eyesight, anglers are less susceptible than others to this phenomenon. With the exception of occasional looks at the fish finder, anglers have little screen time. Their eyes are the better for it.

Fishing environments not only foster less screen time, they also provide situations in which anglers face minimal noise pollution. Exposure to loud noises can result in hearing impairment. Many such noises are mechanical, like sirens or amplified music. These damaging sounds are rare on the water. Anglers would avoid them due to the risk that the unnatural sounds would scatter fish.

Broadcast noises are not the only damaging sounds that anglers are likely to escape. A 2018 study showed that 10 percent of earbud users suffered permanent hearing degradation.[3] A serious angler would not be caught dead wearing earbuds. Earbuds block important environmental stimuli. Away from noises and with ears unencumbered, anglers are distant from common causes of hearing loss.

One more item goes into the avoidance category as it pertains to anglers. Literature indicates that uncovering one's feet can improve a person's sense of touch. The tactile sensations are especially relevant to toddlers and the elderly. I am neither. Still, my own experience would

---

3   Adunka, Oliver. "What you need to know about earbuds and hearing loss." Wexnermedical.osu.edu. January 23 2018. What you need to know about earbuds and hearing loss | Ohio State Medical Center (osu.edu)

verify that indication. Feeling with your toes grasses, rocks, and mud gives a strong sensory connection to outdoor environments.

Although the feet are more sensory than you might think, fishing barefoot may not be a good idea. While some input may be gained from exposed feet on the deck of a boat, the danger present with the surrounding hooks is not worth the risk.

VISUAL

Having listed some don'ts, we will move on to some dos. An attribute that many next-level anglers share is visual acuity. They see tiny movements and minute differences in shade or color. Improved visual acuity is one of the more critical skills to acquire to advance in fishing. It can be achieved through training.

Visual acuity training starts with some very simple physical exercises. The cone of peripheral vision can be widened. The only equipment you need is your thumbs. Spread your arms wide and stick out your thumbs. Keeping your head still, look from your left thumb to your right thumb. Repeat this process for three sets of 10 times each. Performing this eye exercise weekly will expand peripheral vision.

Few consider these in weight training, but the palpebrae muscles near the eye need a regular workout. This is one reason that those who work on screens are reminded to blink. Blinking flexes muscles around the eye, and it keeps the eyes lubricated. Acuity training takes blinking one step further. Experts recommend squeezing your eyes shut. After closing them, vigorously hold them shut for 30 seconds. It will feel like you are scrunching your face. As with other muscle exercises, participants should feel the burn. This burn comes right above your cheeks. Repeat four times and start the cycle again every few days.

After working on peripheral vision and strengthening eye muscles, the next step is train your mind to see details. One entertaining way to start is to watch reruns of *Idiotest* on television. In addition, there are lots of brain games on the market. However, one need not spend money to practice observing details.

One cost-free method is to observe a room. Sit in a quiet place with a wide view of the surrounding space. Take it in. Following the observation, close your eyes and imagine the details of the area. These details should not be limited furniture and artwork placement. Try to recall aspects like textures, trim colors, and shadows. No detail is too small. Spend several minutes on this review. When finished, reopen your eyes. Check your memory. Make sure you saw the pulled green thread on the pillow and the white scratch on the carved foot of the coffee-shaded side table. Recall the placement of the lines from the last vacuum run and the dust on the light bulb. Close your eyes again to try to remember any new intricacies. Sometimes the participant will walk the room with their eyes shut to experience the space while employing other senses. The goal is to try to internalize every single feature. The next week, try a different room.

Indoors spaces are confined, making them manageable for new trainees. In addition, fewer things are moving in a walled space (hopefully). Following training to perceive more details, and lots of practice in so doing, an angler would apply this technique to an outdoor setting.

For a first attempt in the outdoors, focus on an individual tree. A typical brain training request would be to ask the trainee to count the leaves on a tree.

It is an impossible task, but it does focus the mind on edges, curls, points, and color shades to separate one leaf from another. The wind may move some leaves. Bugs, birds, and squirrels could intrude on the developing mental picture. Study of visual details can prepare an angler to perceive small, important natural features ultimately applying the techniques in an expansive natural setting.

After gaining some experience in seeing the details of a natural setting, an angler can take this experience to the water. Every few minutes while fishing, check your peripheral vision and respond to bubbles, ripples, bugs, and birds. Next, close your eyes and visualize the shoreline, the water, the trees, the stumps, and the rocks. Once you see these details, you will recognize the contours and baits most attractive to the bass.

Count the leaves. *Photo by Joe Kinnison.*

HEARING

Just as visual perception can be practiced, hearing discernment can be trained. This training is oriented toward sound differentiation and pattern recognition. Hearing acuity helps an angler perceive the difference between a bird plucking a minnow from the water and a bass attacking an insect on the surface. Those actions have different sounds. Other natural sounds are distinctive as well. Grass moved by wind plays a different chord than grass bent by an animal. The rustle has a disparate quality.

Most musicians train for years to master hearing acuity. Symphonic instruments may sound the same notes but each has a unique tone and resonance. An F-note from a French horn is not the same sound as an F-note from a trumpet. Musicians trying to improve their ear are asked to listen for the part of a particular instrument during a symphonic piece. Being able to isolate sounds improves the hearing acuity.

The same exercise would work for an angler. Listen to your favorite song tracks. If those happen to be popular music, try to listen to the whole song hearing only the bassline. Repeat the process targeting guitar, drums, and background vocals.

As important as sound differentiation is pattern recognition. Mother Nature sets this curriculum. A common prescription for boosting hearing acuity is listening to birdcalls. Birdcalls are often repetitive. However, they are seldom repeated in the same cadence. A bird might make the same call three times in a row, then pause for a minute before sounding a singular call. The length of this pause can change. The rapidity of delivery can change. Tallying the calls and counting the time between them is a recommended method for improving sound pattern perception.

Once experienced with sound quality and sound pattern perception, listen for the natural fishing sounds. Waves hitting the shore have different intensities. Persimmons dropping into the water sound different than kids throwing rocks. The wind has a sound. Gnats have a hum. All of this data is relevant to conditions to which the bass may be reacting.

SMELL

Along with vision and hearing, the sense of smell can be improved through intervention. Different from other senses, however, smell cannot be improved through training exercises. Instead, one's sense of smell can be enhanced through exercise and diet. Physical activity improves the sense of smell. Even a short daily walk is sufficient to help scent detection. The sense of smell improves further with adjustments to diet. If dairy is eliminated from one's diet, mucus production declines. Two small changes to exercise and diet can improve detection of smells.

PROCESSING

Whether concentrating on a visual scene or parsing sounds, anglers realize details by processing those sensory inputs deliberately. The training centers on discerning details amid sensory input. Christiana Bradley calls this meditation. Meditation is one effective technique for getting the brain to accept increased specificity.

Fishing provides plenty of sensations. Over time, anglers learn to perceive relevant details. Experienced anglers have curated their senses.

CHAPTER 8
Versatility:
Changing or fluctuating readily.[1]

Two 15-inch bass separate in a 180-gallon home aquarium. The only occupants flipper away from each other and four feet of water clears between their tail fins. Green plastic artificial ferns rise from the copper and white river rock floor of the tank. Gradually, the fish elevate their heads toward opposite corners, slotting between two fused plates of thick glass. Both fish crack their lips and flare their gills in seeming anticipation.

Two caretakers approach the enclosure from across the floor. Each carries a blue plastic bucket by its wire handle. The caretakers move to opposite corners of the massive basement fish tank, and the buckets are raised to the rim of the enclosure. An effluent of warm water and minnows spills into the aquarium with enough force that the waters momentarily have two distinct blue-gray colors. It looks like the first dissipating bloom from a wetted Easter egg coloring tablet. The minnows tumble, and each bass begins to slurp the baitfish.

Having emptied her bucket, caretaker Pam Martin-Wells steps back to watch the bass feed. She has mischief in her eyes and a big smile on her face. Her mid-length, sandy-colored hair is held back by a visor, giving her clear sight lines to observe the animals. The big bass seem to have a keen sense of the dimensions of their enclosure, the plants, the rocks, the corners. They know all of the hiding places and how to access them. The fish herd their captives. Martin-Wells watches the stalking

---

1   Retrieved November 1, 2020, from https://www.merriam-webster.com/dictionary/versatility

and evaluates the bites. She wants to know which minnows are consumed first. She tries to appreciate the priority given to size, color, and vigor among the hunted.

The action in the tank subsides several minutes later. When conditions normalize, she raises an arm that would make a fitness guru envious, and she knocks on the glass with the knuckle of her forefinger. The bass on her end of the tank freezes and trains an eye on Pam. A moment later, she purposely releases the handle of her two-gallon bucket. The pail drops to the floor, hitting with a *clap*. It tips over and rolls to a stop at its protruding lip. Both bass spook at the noise. Pam flashes another playful smile.

To someone who attributes part of her fishing success to appreciating the brain of the animal, analyzing fish in their own environment is time well spent. The aquarium gives Martin-Wells a chance to do some study of bass headspace. Over time, she witnesses how they feed, how they relate to their environment, and how they relate to one another. It is part of her fishing preparation.

While the tank provides frequent touchpoints, Pam performs occasional fish studies underwater herself. Pam is an accomplished scuba diver, with over 15 dives to her credit. In one of her freshwater dives, she found fascination with seeing how bass relate to cover. On another underwater excursion, she filmed two bass nesting (the video is available on YouTube). In addition to viewing mating, she has accumulated firsthand knowledge of how the fish react to baits, boats, and swimmers. Among the insights, her work has given her an especially acute sense of how bass react to sound.

SOUND

An aquatic environment pays havoc with sound transmission. If you have done much swimming, you have likely experienced that humans hear differently underwater. With our heads submerged, sound waves do not vibrate the ossicles in our ears in that same way that they do so in the air. Instead of activating within our inner ear, sound tends to be absorbed by our skull bones. The muffled, tingly sensation differs from conventional hearing.

Despite the differing source of reception, humans can determine many tones underwater. We can hear sounds ranging between 20 hertz and 1000 hertz. Nearly the entire range of frequencies permeable in the aqueous media is audible to the human ear.

Despite water being their home turf, bass are comparatively less adept. While the science on bass hearing is not precise, researchers are pretty certain that the fish cannot hear anything in frequencies higher than 500 hertz. In addition, it is believed that the fish hear well only the sounds in a range between 60 and 200 hertz. Bass are only likely hearing sounds in about 10 percent of the auditory range available in water. Although the range of sounds that they hear is limited, bass have tested to be highly sensitive to sounds in the 65 to 75 hertz range. This range of vibrations is consistent with sound made by the movements of their prey.

Limited hearing may not necessarily be a detriment for bass. For any animal, it is difficult to find the origin of sound underwater. Any noise is faint relative to the same intensity sound in air. Sound conversion is difficult due to different measurement units for air and water, but as an approximation of the difference, a normal human conversation in the media of air would be inaudible underwater. Second, due to the density of water, sound travels quickly, five times faster than it does in the air. Imagine how long it takes to find the source of an unexpected noise, like someone dropping a plate in the kitchen. Now, have that sound come and go five times faster. Due to low intensity and fast transmission, sound tracking in water is difficult without the aid of electronics.

Not equipped with a good auditory sense, bass respond to unusual noises with a flight instinct. Sensitive to muffled sounds and unable to locate their origin, the bass's innate response is to exit the scene. Experienced anglers teach quiet for exactly this reason. Talking, banging gear, or stomping on a boat deck may scatter the fish. Sounds that transmit through the hull are the ones most likely to alert the fish. Anchors and stringers are usual suspects.

Not only are bass flighty when hearing noise in general, they probably acquire some noise recognition over time. "Bass have a brain and a survival instinct," Pam reminds fellow anglers. The fish has proven to be savvy in both identifying the whine of a trolling motor prop and the whirr of a live well pump. Upon hearing those noises, attacking a bait will not likely be the first thing on their minds.

Pam Martin-Wells fishes with attention to noise. She starts by utilizing her preparation. Sounds emanate from boat traffic and fishing pressure. Avoiding both, Pam finds fishing holes away from the crowd. For example, she located a spring among the grasses in an empty Lake Seminole cove. The quiet, cool burble gushes bass.

Sound suppression aboard begins with equipment. For best results, anything on deck should be secured. Latches and lids are to be fastened. Along with being held fast, gear is best arranged to give the angler some freedom of movement. Pam wants to be able to navigate the deck without kicking something. When she has to move, she steps deliberately.

Along with gear management, careful motor control can lead to stealth. Sound is particularly acute in vegetation and on shallow flats. Especially in these situations, Pam minimizes trolling motor stops and starts. If she has no option other than to use the motor, she will maintain constant direction and speed. Moving the motor would change the frequency of the whir and potentially cause a baffle in the water.

To the extent that she can do so, Pam takes advantage of wind. She will position her boat upwind and let the breeze move the boat. If she needs to control the speed, she can do so with a sea anchor, which is a small parachute that deploys in the water and provides drag.

A quiet approach to fishing does not only apply to the shallows. In fishing deeper ledges and channels, most anglers use the motor to try to maintain position. If Pam can locate either a brush pile or a relatively stationary school of baitfish, she will fix her position by slowly releasing the anchor. Having seen for herself how sensitive bass can be to noises, Pam employs sound suppression as a competitive advantage.

SHAKY HEADS

For an angler sensitive to sound, Martin-Wells favors a quiet bait, a shaky head worm. The shaky head is a smaller lure, traditionally fished with light weights. Although the lure does not chatter, rattle, or agitate, it does make a dull tap in the frequency attractive to bass when the bait falls to the bottom. This quiet bait works well in a more crowded and active body of water.

Shaky heads mimic two separate natural behaviors. Crawfish clicking around a lake or river bottom take a defensive posture when big fish swim nearby. They sink their tail into bottom structure and array their pincers upward. Since the shaky head soft plastic element flutters above the weight, it can appear as a crayfish in a defensive posture. Wholly separate from the crayfish conception, a shaky head can look like small fish feeding on the bottom. Snorkelers and divers have likely seen small fish suctioning food off rocks and corals. When a fish is feeding in this way, they often have their tails angled toward the surface. Shaky head rigs can also look like small fish flapping their tails to maintain position near a food source on the bottom. Bass will eat almost anything, so they may not care whether they think they see a crayfish defending or a baitfish feeding. Because of its similarities to several types of forage, the shaky head can be a devastatingly effective bait.

Assemble a shaky head by threading a small plastic worm onto a purpose-built jig head. The jig heads made explicitly for shaky head fishing have an eyelet for the fishing line connection in either the 10 o'clock or 12 o'clock position on the jig head ball. Shaky head weights can be either metallic or they can be painted. Pam prefers the painted version with simulated eyes on either side. The paint job can make the lure look more like feeding baitfish. Immediately up the hook from the ball, a shaky head has either a short spiral of wire or a nub that looks like an arrowhead split down its axis and turned backward. The screw or the nub is used to secure the tip of an artificial worm.

As for the worm portion of the lure, plastic worms come in multiple sizes. Anglers use many variations on shaky head rigs. Worms range from four to 10 inches in length. A four-inch plastic worm is the traditional combination with the jig head. Shorter worms seem to work best when using the rig for pressured bass.

Artificial worms have different properties: spiral tails, flukes, tapers, and sticks. Some plastics float. The floating aspect is particularly

Shaky head presentation with four-inch green pumpkin worm. *Photo by Joe Kinnison.*

important for shaky head presentations. Trick worms are built to have a hollow section in the middle of the bait. This hollow area holds air, and the air causes the worm to float. A floating worm enhances the shaking action above the jig head. As a caution to anglers assembling shaky heads, finesse worms and other poured varieties of soft plastic baits do not float.

If navigating the worm varieties is not complicated enough, plastic worms also come in a myriad of colors: green pumpkin, watermelon red, and june bug, to name a few of the more popular ones.

Red is a default color for soft plastics. Bass do not see the color well, and red spectrum colors disappear first as the lure sinks in the water column. Diversifying from red, her color selection depends on the bottom structure and water clarity.

Dark bottoms call for dark colors. Green pumpkin looks natural on a silted bottom. Vegetation or green shaded water triggers use of the watermelon shade. Stained and silted water shifts her choice to purple-toned june bug or an emerald blue.

Having seen plastic worms underwater with her own goggled eyes, Pam observes that below 25 feet, every color of lure looks the same. They all read black. When she is fishing deep ledges and channels, Pam skips the natural color pretense, and she uses black plastic worms.

The spiral from the jig head is threaded into the tip of a plastic worm. The body of the plastic worm is then stretched flat and fitted over the barb of the trailing hook. Covering the barb makes a shaky head weedless, which enhances the lure's versatility. In most cases, two or three inches of worm extends past a typical 3/0 gap hook. This dangling section of the worm shakes, wiggles, and flutters while the lure rests on the bottom.

Fishing a shaky head rig can have as much versatility as the rig itself. Pam will normally present the shaky head rig using several different methods of retrieve. From her first casts, she will wait for the rig to hit bottom. The fall rate of a lure will vary greatly by the type of line used and the temperature of the water. As a gross approximation, it takes about one second for a quarter-ounce lure to descend one foot in a water column. If she is fishing in 10 feet of water, Pam would wait about 10 seconds for the lure to settle. Once the lure hits bottom, Pam will raise the tip of her rod from three o'clock to one o'clock to pull the lure up from the bottom. She will then quickly return to her start position, allowing the lure to crash back into the lake or river floor. Continuing this cycle, Pam will bounce the lure back to the boat, or until she gets a strike. The bouncing movement attracts attention, reproduces the thudding sound of the lure impacting the bottom, and looks like scampering prey.

Should the bouncing prove ineffective, Pam will change tactics. Sometimes she uses a steady retrieve to drag the shaky head lure along the bottom. At other times, she keeps the lure where it lands and shakes it by making short back-and-forth sweeps with her rod. If those methods do not produce, she elevates the lure a few feet off the bottom and swims it back to the boat. Pam is a big believer in versatility. She has seen for herself that bass are smart and that they quickly learn lures and patterns. To coax bites, she knows that she needs to show them something new. With the shaky head, she can show them new jig heads, new worm styles, new worm lengths, and different retrieves.

SEARCH BAITS

Before Pam can employ her shaky head configurations, she has to find the fish. Search baits help accomplish the task. Search baits are movement baits. They are employed to probe suspected bass habitats. Aggressive fish react to the baits. These strikes often reveal the presence of fish in the area.

Bass move from hour to hour and from day to day. Discovering the location of the fish is an exercise in versatility. Next-level anglers will sample topography such as flats, points, mini points, and humps. Depth, speed, and direction are also varied. An assortment of actions is a feature of a search bait.

Search Bait—Squarebill Summer Sexy Shad. *Courtesy of Strike King.*

Pam's favorite search bait is a squarebill crankbait. The lure looks like a minnow, and it has a straight plastic scoop by its mouth. The nearly half-inch scoop is sufficient to drive the lure as deep as five feet. It can also be fished shallower by varying speed and rod angle. The straight front edge enables the crankbait to bump off submerged rocks and trees. Deflections cause the reaction strikes. A collection of those strikes reveals the orientation of the fish.

The squarebill can be retrieved at a fast pace, enabling the angler to scour terrain. Alternatively, it can be twitched on the surface, acting as a topwater lure. Pam generally frowns on using a topwater lure as a search bait, so she would not try this for long. Not only can the squarebill be twitched, it can also be retrieved with a succession of reels and stops. The squarebill is versatile.

Once she starts getting bites, Pam will try to establish a pattern. A pattern can be specific to lure placement. It can be to cast lures up against tie walls. It could be twitching three times and then retrieving a lure. A pattern can be a color, like yellow.

Patterns can be specific to location. Fish could be several feet back from the tip of a point. They could be halfway upstream from a creek mouth. On a given day, fish might suspend main channel ledges at a consistent depth.

Patterns can also be specific to cover. Fish can relate to a particular branch on a particular kind of fallen tree. The cover need not be natural. Fish could position themselves underneath props of docked pontoon boats.

Using search baits, next-level anglers first discover fish. Second, they derive a pattern. With a pattern identified, Pam will switch to a more subtle presentation like a shaky head.

COOSA RIVER

Pam Martin-Wells has a soft spot in her heart for the Coosa River system. The region has become her home away from home. As testament to her affinity for the Northern Alabama tributary, her beloved dog is named Coosa. As for the river, she knows the features and the flows.

After a predawn goodbye to a longtime friend in Gadsden, Alabama, Pam makes the short drive to Coosa Landing. She and another angler occupy two of the four launch ramps. The 125-slot parking lot has three truck and trailer spots already occupied. Beams of warm light are angling out the windows of the bait shop across the street. The early fall air smells of wet mulch.

On a walk back from the parking lot to the dock, Pam checks her watch. According to the published schedule from Alabama Power, the H. Neely Henry Dam opens a single spillway at 7 o'clock a.m. The H. Neely Henry Dam has four spillways. As power needs in the region rise, spillways open

Pam Martin-Wells and Coosa. *Selfie.*

to turn generators. During the summer, it is not unusual for three or four spillways to be open. When this occurs, the pull is too strong for angling. In the spring and fall shoulder seasons, one or two spillways will open, and only for a few hours each day. The soft current created by a single flume creates ideal fishing conditions on the river. Pam sits on the edge of the pier, lowers herself into her boat, and fires the engine. As the sky starts to pink from the impending sunrise, she drives toward the dam five miles downstream.

Pam arrives above the dam, and she positions her boat near a fallen cottonwood at the shoreline. With the flash of a red light and a claxon sound, motion begins at the dam. Pam double-checks her battery and engages her trolling motor. She will not shut it off for several hours, as she putters through several bends in the river on her way back to Gadsden.

Coosa River. *Copyright 2021 Garmin Ltd or its subsidiaries.*

The current quickly activates the fish. Bass holding on the river ledges swim to the protection of current breaks and shoreline cover. Pam catches her first largemouth of the day almost immediately.

Pam makes slow progress up the river against the broadening current. She picks off an aggressive bass up-current from a tangled mass of tree trunks. She sends another lure past the protected eddies to the less-aggressive fish. Largemouth bass remain her top target until she reaches the top of H. Neely Henry Lake.

Pam tracks the water flow as it advances north. As the sun rises above the arm-stretching shoreline trees, she changes tactics. Still mimicking baitfish sucked by the flow, she moves deeper. Spotted bass become more prevalent up lake.

Pam takes a couple of hours mirroring the spillway current as it makes its way to Gadsden. It can be hard to maintain pace and switch species, but Pam says it's worth it. Take her word for it. She won the WBT events on H. Neely Henry in 2006 and 2009. She finished second in 2008.

SANTEE COOPER LAKES

Pam is equally adept fishing at rivers and lakes. When it comes to lakes, the Santee Cooper Lakes are a local favorite. The lakes have unique freshwater forage, famous cover, and occasional current.

Lake Marion and Lake Moultrie were created in 1941 as part of a plan to create a waterway from coastal Charleston to interior Columbia, South Carolina. The 162-mile trek opened its full length in 1943. It boasted the greatest water level change in a hydraulic lock at its time, 80 feet. That Pinopolis Lock sits at the base of 60,000-acre Lake Moultrie, the eastern lake in the chain. Both lakes are large, but Lake Marion is about twice Lake Moultrie's size in acre-feet.

The shared water is stained, and it has a yellowish hue that announces plant life. Both lakes have live standing trees in their shallows and submerged shoreline grasses. In still conditions, the lakes have a musky smell, a carryover from the swamps that they flooded. The surrounding area is generally flat and forested, and only a few sections of the coastline are developed.

When created, Lake Marion flooded a historic swamp. Today, the northern end of the lake is called the Stumphole Swamp. It has acres of flooded cypress trees interspersed with laydowns and tree remnants. The tangle of vegetation is thick. Stumphole is easier to navigate with a kayak than a bass boat, but significant parts of it are accessible to anglers one way or another. It is fertile bass fishing ground.

Lake Marion holds the credentials for largemouth bass fishing. The state record bass was caught on that lake only eight years after the lake was created. The 16 pound, two-ounce fish has been tied but never beaten. The Bassmaster Elite series held a tour stop at Santee Cooper in 2020.

FORAGE, VARIETY, AND CURRENT

The path inland from the ocean provides a route for both lakes to have an unexpected natural forage base, blueback herring. Herring is atypical forage for a freshwater lake, as the species is mostly a saltwater fish. However, blueback herring is one of the few subspecies that can tolerate brackish and fresh water. Bluebacks do swim up many rivers along the east coast, but they seldom go as far inland as the nearly 30 miles from Charleston to Santee Cooper's Moncks Corner.

While some fish species dig into bottom structures to lay their eggs, herring have a different approach. They drop their eggs from higher in the water column. The eggs are coated with a substance which makes them stick to the surface of rocks and stumps. With these eggs exposed, they become food for other species of fish, who suck them off their resting spots. Lake Marion and Lake Moultrie will have thousands of fish feeding from the bottom with their tails aimed toward the surface. Pam's shaky head lures are designed to mimic this behavior.

The large forage base makes the Santee Cooper Lakes one of the great sport fisheries in the country. The sister lakes have produced world records in both channel catfish (58 lbs) and redear sunfish (5.5 lbs). State-record white perch, blue catfish, black crappie, longnose gar, and largemouth bass were caught on the lakes. Anglers target a wide variety of species, but catfishing is most prominent.

Bass anglers have options. Not only do the lakes hold sizable largemouth bass, but also the striped bass population is growing. While regulations prohibit fishing for stripers during the summer months, anglers can target them in the shoulder seasons. With a limited season, the "stripers" are getting large. Average weights exceed 10 pounds. A good-sized catch at Santee Cooper is a 25-pounder.

The silver-scaled stripers are an adapted saltwater species. Some were trapped behind the dam when the lakes were created. The fish were not expected to survive once confined to freshwater, but they did. They actually grew and began to reproduce. Accidental success in Lake Moultrie led to these fish being introduced into freshwater lakes around the country.

Different from the shallow-dwelling largemouths, striped bass typically suspend deep within lakes, down 20 feet or more. Stripers are often caught while trolling, which is a method of trailing lures behind a moving boat. The angler covers a large stretch of water, running lures, like spoons and crankbaits, nearby suspending fish. One of the recommended guides, Santee Cooper Charters, fishes for stripers exclusively. Lake Moultrie's 70- to 80-foot depths provide habitat for the striped bass.

The lakes have been in the news in recent years, but not for their prolific fishing. The reporting has related to the power plants on their shores. The Santee Cooper Lakes generate hydropower, with more than 50,000 cubic feet per second of water rushing through the spillways each summer day. When the spillways at the Cross Generating Station open, a water circulation opens throughout the lakes.

Santee Cooper is not only the name of the lake system, it is the name of the local electric utility company. The aging of the utility infrastructure is causing some issues with the lake. The power plant was part of a large project to replace the coal and hydro combination with a new nuclear generating unit. That nuclear project experienced design problems and cost overruns. It was shelved a few years ago. The financial loss from sunk costs was debilitating to the utility. With the future of the power plant in limbo, the future of the Santee Cooper Lakes is uncertain. Draining the lakes is one possibility that local officials have discussed should the local power plants shut down. However, a new power contract from Century Aluminum may have stabilized the situation for the near term.

The spillways often open at midday, and the current can extend the fishing hours beyond the normal morning and evening times. The fish have difficulty holding position during a current flow, so they mass near anything that disrupts the water movement. Rocks, stumps, and piers all serve that purpose. Pockets of relatively placid water behind such impediments to the current are called eddies. Fish spend less energy holding in the eddies. When bass venture into the flow, they tend to face currents. Knowing this orientation helps anglers position lures upstream.

During the current flows, Pam will drift the Diversion

Pam Martin-Wells landing a bass. *Selfie.*

Canal from Lake Marion to Lake Moultrie. This narrow strip of water has relatively strong flow and ample eddies in which fish hide.

The canal enters Lake Moultrie and diffuses from its channel. South of the canal begins a long flat. Pam will fish underwater features including mounds and old foundations that are dotted along the flat. Off the south edge of the shallows opens another channel, formerly an open water gap through the Moorfield Swamp. The channel extends deeper water from the main lake nearly all of the way to the shore. This gap provides a pathway for circulating bass. Channel edges can be productive for fishing throughout the day.

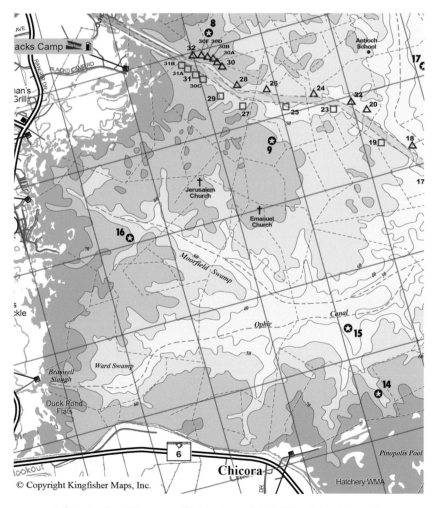

Lake Moultre Waterproof Map, Item #312. Kingfisher Maps, Inc.
Used with permission.

Toward the body of the lake, the old swamp gives way to much deeper water. If you do not find the Hall of Fame angler on the channels or the flats, check around the deep edges for a scuba-diving flag. Where you find her bubbles, you will find the fish.

VISITING

Towns around the Santee Cooper Lakes welcome fishing tourists. Moncks Corner is the closest boat launch to Charleston. It has a lakeside park above the Lake Moultrie dam complete with a boat launch and two concrete piers. The town is tourist-friendly, and it has several bait shops. The surrounding area has an "Old South" feel. Nearby plantations are worth a visit.

For those who do not mind driving a little farther, Black's Camp is located on the south edge of the Diversion Canal. Black's is a fish camp in the true sense. Its prominent feature is a 25-peg display board on which anglers can hang their daily catch. The spot is popular for pictures. You may have to wait your turn, but you will enjoy the dock talk as you wait.

Many guides work out of Black's Camp. In fact, so many guides launch their boats here that visiting anglers can select guides specific to their targeted fish species. The 18-slip marina can be over-full at dawn, and the fish cleaning station can have a wait midday.

Select Santee Cooper Fishing Guide Services

Fishing with Brett Mitchell	803-379-7029	brettmitchell@bellsouth.net
Santee Cooper Bass Country	803-478-7289	email@inkydavis.com
Santee Cooper Charters	843-729-2212	truman@homesc.com

Lodging at Black's Camp consists of motel-type apartments, cabins, and camping sites. It is a no-frills fish camp, which seems suited to the hard-core fishing vibe of Santee Cooper. As an example of the degree of dedication to fishing of this area, they actually advertise that rooms have power supplies sufficient to recharge boat batteries. As fish camps go, Black's Camp is well outfitted. They have a restaurant on-site. It is a beer and burger place that serves to salve tired anglers.

MULTIPLICITY

Pam's strength as an angler is her versatility. As with other next-level qualities, like structure, physiology, and acuity, versatility is a skill that can be enhanced. Broadening one's fishing perspective starts with in-depth study of aspects such as color. Gains in knowledge are applied through experimentation and ingrained through improvisation. There is a right way to employ both.

Get-on-the-water-and-go types of anglers will not like to hear this, but more versatility starts with greater familiarity with equipment and lore. It starts with study. Bass fishing is blessed with instructional materials. Magazine articles and videos are plentiful. Use them.

Growing your working knowledge of color, for example, adds to your available choice set. Knowing that red works best in shallows, and blue works best deep is not sufficient. Likewise, understanding that flash and fleck work best on cloudy days and solids work best in the sun will not be enough. Learn which lure colors are likely to work best at different depths of your lake or river. Adjust for water clarity, forage, and fishing pressure.

As with color, investigating lures that are new to you can add dimensions to your angling. If you have never heard of a chatterbait, procure one and try it. If you have never caught a fish with a mixed bladed spinner bait, tie one on and keep casting until you secure a bite. Once experienced with more lure types, an amateur can become more versatile by casting lures in what they consider to be atypical situations.

On those days when you catch your limit early, change it up. Put away the comfortable baits and try something new. Stylistic experimentation can add options and increase confidence. Switching from power to finesse, or vice versa, would broaden your tool set. It might also produce something distinctive. Such a style adaptation may yield in an unusual presentation. Surprising fish with a different depth, speed, or cadence may make them more inclined to bite. You never know when you might need a changeup.

Experimentation is where the "what" meets the "how." In a 2009 paper, MITSloan recommended experimentation as a method to improve decision making.[2] Running a real-world test is likely to provide more substantive information than debating and discussing how a customer, in this case a fish, might respond to a new stimulus.

Modifying that guidance for angling, if you cannot decide between a white or a blue crankbait, in turns, throw both. See what happens. The fish will tell you which they prefer. In the same vein, go fishing on a bad weather day. For example, set out after the passing of a cold front. Slow retrieval speeds, downsize baits, or add scents. The fish will indicate a preference, revealing what the angler might employ the next time a bite gets slow.

While experimentation often leads to data for better decisions, improvisation makes the best use of versatility. According to a Wharton interview with author Bob Kulhan, improv leads to open-mindedness.[3] Anglers willing to improvise accept alternative scenarios and twists to their understood reality. It helps them process information.

Improv helps openness by imposing a structure for ideation. Improvisation is not just the act of winging it. Improvisation, as practiced by actors, comedians, and musicians, has parameters and orders of operation. Entertainers do not generally free form. They are taught improv.

Actors first learning improv are given games to prompt quick thinking. They may be asked to begin a sentence with the last word of a preceding sentence, or to begin a new statement with a progressing letter of the alphabet. "Are you going to the store?" would be followed by, "Be there in 30 minutes," and "Can you get some kumquats?"

As improv participants progress, they are presented with a setting, a scene, and a story prompt. With those raw materials, they call upon an assortment of patterned behaviors. One entertainer may start playing with how she moves, adding an unusual walk or a tic. Another

---

2   Luca, Michael and Bazerman, Max. *MIT Management Review.* June 4, 2020. Want to Make Better Decisions? Start Experimenting.

3   "How improv methods from comedy can lift business performance." knowledge@ wharton. April 9, 2017.

entertainer might choose to be transformed by the scene, having an unusual reaction to the set by noticing a picky detail.

Exploding a detail from a scene might be a good starting point for an improv artist. It is also a good launching point for an improv angler. One could get obsessed with rounded, mossy rocks right below the waterline as an unusual feature of the setting. Drawing fish from that setting detail might prescribe lure selections or presentations.

Next to exploding a detail, an improv technique called "Yes, and" might fit a fishing trip. The exercise calls for an actor to accept a premise, agree to it, and add something . In fishing parlance, an angler might accept that ripping deep diving, crayfish-pattered crankbaits is picking up bass in lake pockets. He or she might fish those areas with the prescribed gear and follow on with, say, casting green pumpkin swim jigs with craw trailers into the same lake pockets.

Improvising by choice is useful preparation for times when improvising is the only way. Although many anglers have extensive tackle boxes filled with dozens of lures, it is still possible to be lacking the right lure for the moment. I have witnessed two anglers in the same boat fishing green plastic worms with far different results. One angler had four-inch worms. He was slaying the bass. One angler had only six-inch worms. He did not get a single bite. In a situation such as that, improvisation can build versatility. Soft plastic lures can be trimmed. After cutting the plastic worms, they worked fine. Missing the perfect bait, improvisation may save the fishing day. Tuning lures with weights, rattles, cuts, and splices is well within bounds of acceptable practice.

By experimenting and improvising, an angler can become more versatile. Data gathering and improvisation routines can be taught. Now a college educator, Martin-Wells is instructing the next generation on fishing versatility.

CHAPTER 9
Stewardship:
The careful and responsible management of something entrusted to one's care.[1]

Good stewardship starts from the moment the bass bites. Correctly setting a hook and managing the landing deliver the fish to the angler in the best possible condition. A few tricks ensure that even the most deep-set hooks can be removed to preserve the fish. Handling and releasing to reanimate the bass give it the best chance for a return to normal function.

HOOK SET

Occasionally, a fish will hook itself. The animal may bite so hard that it clamps on to a barb. It might put enough steady tension on the line to run the point of a hook through its lip. But, this is not the norm. In most cases, the angler must set the hook.

Knowing that action is required on their part, anglers can get zealous in their hook setting. Amateur anglers will squat their legs when they feel a fish nibble. From a coiled position, hook sets can turn into explosive movements. Full extension ends up with the angler's arms extended over her head. Such a set delivers a wallop, which can yank the impaled fish to the surface.

---

1   Retrieved November 1, 2020, from https://www.merriam-webster.com/dictionary/stewardship

Although brute force will secure the biting bass, a few pounds of pressure are all of the force necessary. Instead of involving arms and legs, a flick of the wrist delivers sufficient power.

Hook setting is properly accomplished using one of two methods, tight line or slack. Using the tight line method, an angler applies a moment of firm resistance when the bass is moving a lure. The slack method is employed when fish are proving sensitive to resistance. An angler lets a few feet of sag in the line. When convinced that the bass has taken the bait, she whips the loose line taut.

While keeping the line straight, the angler lowers the rod tip in anticipation of the tight line set. Timing is everything with this hook set. The angler must not reveal herself to the fish through line pressure. On the other hand, the angler awaits some feedback to indicate that the bass has done more than bump the lure. Once the bass first nibbles, an angler using the tight line method would lean in the direction of the fish and reel in the line. The line would stay taut, but it would not drag the bitten lure toward the angler. With the fish engaged, the angler raises the rod tip from close to the water level to a point above her head. This motion is to be quick and singular.

The slack approach is self-descriptive. Having detected a bite, the angler permits a few feet of slack to develop in the line. This may come naturally as a result of the fish swimming the lure. If not, the angler can provide slack by lowering the rod tip. Slack may permit the fish a second bite or it may keep the fish from discovering the angler. The hook set with slack is much more dramatic than the set using a tight line. The angler raises the rod tip at once in a snap motion. The slack is collected, and force is transferred down the line to the hook. This method generates a deeper hook set, and it often shocks the fish.

Hook set does not stop with penetration of the barb. With either method, the line must remain tight after the initial set. A quick spin of the reel often follows hook set. With the fish under control, the angler begins playing the fish.

PLAYING A FISH

Once a fish has taken the bait, next-level angling skills really come into play. Tugging a fish either to the shore or to the side of a boat is seldom a successful strategy. Powerful fish can thwart the effort, and the method puts stress on fishing gear. Instead of taking a chance on the vagaries of fish and equipment, a gentle approach has a higher success rate. The fish is best guided away from hazards while it tires from resisting pressure on the line.

As simple direction for playing a fish, try employing two rules. When a fish is swimming away from you, and that may be either linear or deeper, do not reel. Let the drag from the reel, or the resistance of your thumb against the spool if using a baitcaster, slow its escape. However, if a fish is swimming toward you, raise your rod tip and recover fishing line as quickly as you can.

Anyone who has landed a large bass knows that at some point during the retrieve, the bass will figure out the origin of the pressure on the line. Most big bass have been caught numerous times. Bass are smart creatures with a survival instinct. The accumulated experience can thwart less-prepared anglers. Large bass will rush the source of pressure. They will try to generate slack in the line and loosen the hook. Managing these moments often determines whether or not the angler ultimately lands the fish. Few reels recover line fast enough to offset a rush. Line tension can be maintained by raising the rod or, in the alternate, shifting the rod in the opposite direction of the oncoming fish. Whatever the juxtaposition, maintaining line tension is the key. A secondary goal is to coax the fish to a path that is something other than parallel with the angler. Using the rod to shift the fish, even a few degrees opposed to the eyelets, gives the angler more control. Once the angler withstands the rush, the fish may be played to the shore or the boat.

Use the pump and reel method to land a bass. As the fish is tiring, an angler should draw it closer by raising the rod tip above her head. From that position, the angler reels line while lowering the rod toward the direction of the fish. Upon completing this cycle, the angler repeats it by raising the rod tip to draw the fish closer once again. The angler alternates pumping and reeling until the fish is in sight. At that point, a determination is made as to whether the fish is sufficiently exhausted to be landed. If not, the angler permits short runs against pressure from the reel drag. Hurrying this process risks the fish making a sudden surge and breaking the now short string of line.

HANDLING

Watch a televised fishing tournament sometime. You cannot help but notice how the professional anglers handle the fish that they catch. Unless the fish jumps near the boat, which enables the angler to swing the fish aboard, anglers lower a hand into the water and grasp the fish. Some go bare-handed, and some use gloves. Bass may be captured by the lip or the belly or with a net.

Although many tournaments do not allow nets, nets are perfectly acceptable for recreational anglers. Nets do have drawbacks, however. Nets often tangle with free hooks on a lure, the hooks not sunk into the fish. These hook-to-net snags can increase the time required to extricate the fish. Such delays can do damage to the animal. Those nets constructed using wide-gapped rubber mesh have fewer drawbacks. The rubber mesh does not cling to hooks, and the wider space between threads is more forgiving. Rubber has an additional advantage of removing less of the fish's protective slime coat. Next-level anglers who choose to use nets employ those with rubber mesh.

For those who would prefer to use their hands, free hand is fine, and gloves are permitted. However, tournament fishing does impose some limits on capturing the fish. Anglers are prohibited from pinning fish. The animals may not be held against the side of the boat or trapped against the shoreline. Likewise, they cannot be grappled against the angler's body. A fish must be plucked from the water with a single hand.

Grabbing a bass by its lower lip gives the angler leverage to control the fish and lift it onto the shore or into a boat. Executing this grip necessitates the fish being within arm's length. The fish must also be sufficiently tired from its fight that it can be held in place with only a single hand on a rod.

To grip the lip of the fish, anglers can start by manipulating the fish's mouth open. Line tension on the lure can spread the lips. The fish's lower lip is pinched between the angler's thumb and the base of her curled forefinger. This method is the least harmful to the fish, but downsides exist for the angler.

Bass have teeth. They are small, inward-facing, and needle-like. It is hard to avoid these teeth when lipping a bass, although the best practice is for the angler to pinch the floor of the mouth behind the row of teeth. With a moving animal, still in the water and hooked, the teeth are hard to avoid. Avoiding them is not absolutely necessary. A minor negative from pinching teeth instead of jaw is that the angler's thumb is often roughed up. This condition is called "bass thumb." It is quite common, and it is manifest as rough skin and occasionally some redness on the appendage.

A more significant problem than aiming the thumb is protecting against impalement. Bass often shake when grabbed. That shaking has the potential to create contact between the lure and the angler's hand. Many anglers who make a practice of landing fish by the lip have made hospital trips to have hooks removed from their arms and hands.

A safer route for anglers has some consequences for the fish. Bass tend to still when they are held by their bellies. Anglers can take advantage of this reaction to land fish. Again, the hooked fish is brought within arm's length of the angler. While controlling the fish with the rod in one hand, the angler reaches the other hand into the water cupping under the fish. The angler grasps the body of the fish just below the pectoral fins. Squeezing the animal gently in his palm, the angler controls and lifts the fish. Cupping the belly is safer for the angler. There are no hooks and no teeth to contend with. However, it is less safe for the fish. Bass are covered with a protective mucus called a slime coat. Handing the fish in this manner rubs off some of the slime coat. Absent portions of the protective layer, the fish are more susceptible to disease.

Nets and grips have pitfalls. With those issues, anglers may be tempted to land fish by lifting it by the fishing line. As indicated previously, this practice is encouraged in situations where the bass jumps from the water near the shoreline or boat. Landing an airborne bass actually has an official term, "swinging." With a fish above the water, it has upward momentum and little drag, making stress on the fishing gear minimal. If swinging a fish ashore, for the safety of the animal, contact with the ground or the boat deck should be minimized. Flopping on the deck can inflict damage on the fish.

HOOK REMOVAL

Anglers do their best to set hooks into the soft tissues near the mouth of a bass. As much as anglers try to prevent it, sometimes fish swallow the lure. A fish might suck in a lure in one large gulp. If not the bass, an angler might err. Waiting too long for confirmation of a bite is a common mistake. Next-level anglers acquire the skills to save the fish in these instances.

Single hooks, often holding soft plastic baits, are usually the hooks deepest set. These hooks are recoverable, even when they have disappeared as much as halfway down a fish's gullet. Holding the animal by its lower lip, anglers should first try to remove the hook in a conventional way. Having a forceps, a pliers, or a hook-removing instrument greatly aids the effort. With an instrument, put pressure on the base of the hook at the wound site to extract the barb.

If a hook cannot be removed accessing it from the mouth, it can often be retrieved from the bottom-up, through the gills. Two methods are often successful using this gill-side entry.

First, the rounded part of the hook can be pinched in the hook-removing instrument and pulled downward through a gap in the gills. Often changing the angle from which one is trying to free the barb releases the hook. The hook is then pulled free down through the gills. Once disconnected from the fish, the hook can be lifted out of the mouth by gently tugging the fishing line to clear the hook through the gills and out of the mouth.

If pulling the base of the hook downward into the free space between the gills does not free the barb, attempt a second option. Again using a hook remover, enter the mouth cavity through the gills. Pinch the hook in the instrument and twist the instrument 90 degrees, causing the curved bottom of the hook to face upward toward the open mouth. Carefully remove the instrument from the gill, and reenter through the mouth. With the hook upside-down now in the mouth cavity, some force should remove the embedded barb and extract the hook through the mouth. While accessing a swallowed hook through the gills is often a successful method of removal, it does not work in every instance.

Removing a swallowed hook through the gills can take time. Thankfully, anglers have some time to execute the removal task. A bass can persist outside of the water for about 15 minutes. Although 15 minutes is an average survival time, the range is quite wide. Times vary from 4 to 20 minutes depending on conditions. Once hook removal efforts exceed 10 minutes, the fish is likely experiencing duress. It is advisable to swim the fish. Put it back into the water for a few minutes. Let it swim and breathe. Resume the hook removal effort after some recovery time.

It would be normal for attempted removal of a deep-set hook to cause the bass to bleed. A little blood is okay, but heavy bleeding likely indicates that the fish cannot be saved. For a hemorrhaging fish, abandon the hook extraction effort. Either keep the fish or cut the line and set it free. If freed, it will likely perish.

Sometimes a hook cannot be extracted. In those cases, a hook can be left in a fish. The freed fish will attempt to remove the hook itself. It will scrape against rocks, shells, and branches to work against the hook. For hooks stuck in the mouth area, fish are often successful in shedding the hook. Most accomplish the task within a few days. This timing is especially true if the hook remains attached to a lure due to a fishing line breaking. Hooks that are deeply imbedded are a different story. Some fish can live with it, guiding prey around the obstruction. The fish may not be able to dislodge it, but longer term, hooks do deteriorate. They rust, and they bend. It could take a season, but a hook will eventually weather to the point where it becomes likely to fall out. Giving a bass a chance to adapt improves the odds of survival over a lengthy hook extraction. If hook removal is not possible in the survival time window, using a wire cutter to clip as much of the hook as accessible will speed the degradation process.

Even next-level anglers have the fish swallow a hook from time to time. Learning how to extract hooks through the gills, paying careful attention to time, increases the odds of saving one's catch.

RELEASING

Releasing a fish is something of a controversial subject. Many disagree on whether to do it, and a subset disagree on how to do it. Catch and release has been the recommended fishing practice for several decades. Partially as a result of the quantity of released bass, many lakes have developed over-population problems. Conditions with too many mouths and not enough food have stunted growth within fish communities. Some naturalists now wonder whether releasing small bass is in the best interest of the overall fishery. It is a case of the good of one fish may not outweigh the needs of the many. Where regulations permit, catch and keep is the emerging sentiment among recreational anglers. However, that view has opposition.

Those that prefer to release their catch have a dispute within their ranks. The disagreement is over how to handle fish and with what equipment to do so. Nets, hands, gloves, and towels all enter the conversation. Views may contrast, but the joint goal is to ensure the health of a fish returned to the water.

A point on which most agree is that releasing a bass without ever removing it from the water provides the best outcome for the fish. Once a fish has been played to shoreline or to the side of a boat, most anglers can discern whether or not the fish is a keeper. One can usually tell if a fish is likely to fulfill regulatory slot limits. In addition, the extent to which the size is likely to improve one's stringer can often be determined visually. If a decision to release a fish can be readily made, keeping it at least partially in the water is the best solution for the long-term health of the fish.

Releasing a fish in the water necessitates a few gymnastics on the part of the angler. Anglers should control the fish either by grasping the lower lip or by cradling the belly. In either case, the fish should be on top of the water with at least part of its body above the surface. With the hand opposite the one holding the fish, the angler would use a hook-removing tool to reach into its mouth and extract the lure. Using a tool in these situations minimizes the contact between the angler and the fish. Remove the hook. Keeping the fish under control, discard the hook-removing tool and clear the lure from the area.

Once removing the hook, the next step in releasing a fish is to get water flowing through its gills. The fish may be tired after the fight, and it may have inhaled air during the retrieve. If the body of water that you are fishing has current, face the captured fish into the current. The flow of the water should pass through the gills and revive the fish.

To reengage the gills in the absence of water movement, often an angler must clear the fish's mouth area. Those anglers who have been using the "grip the lip" technique for controlling the fish need to transition to cupping the belly. Often changing the hand grasping the fish is the easiest way to swap this hold. To cup the belly, place a rounded hand under the torso behind the gill slits, being careful not to trap the fins.

With the fish held by the belly, the angler should position her free hand to secure the fish's tail. Once a hold on the tail is established, the angler loosens, but does not release, her hold on the belly.

Most times, a fish will swim away once the hold on its torso is relaxed. For moments when the fish does not escape, the angler should check for movement of the gills. Motion in the gill slots indicates that the fish is breathing normally. That is a good sign for ultimate release. If the gills are moving, give the fish a bit more time. After another minute of revival time, the next step would be to wiggle the tail. Sometimes providing that motion gives the fish enough animation to swim.

Again, releasing the fish while keeping it in the water provides the best outcome for the animal. Such releases are not always possible. When a fish is fully landed before ultimately being released, controversy can start. Use of fabrics is a main point of contention in handling of a fish. Representative of the argument, the Nebraska DNR discourages the wearing of gloves when handling and releasing fish, and they reject outright using towels to hold the animals while lures are disconnected.

To the contrary, the US National Park Service okays rubberized gloves for handling fish, and they permit use of wetted towels for containing caught fish prior to release.

Use gloves. Avoid gloves. Employ a wet towel. Refrain from using a towel. These may sound like small points, but advocates hold passionate positions on the subjects. The debate is over the degree to which these items remove the protective slime coat from the fish. Most agree that dry towels and fabric gloves, when pressed against a fish, absorb parts of the slime coat. No one recommends dry fabrics. Wet towels and gloves have supporters for purposes of keeping the landed animal damp. Rubberized gloves, which are less absorbent than fabric gloves, have more advocates.

With both government agencies and well-meaning anglers on both sides of this issue, professional fishing tours have a clear point of view on these subjects. Gloves are approved for use by tour anglers, and many professional anglers use gloves for release. Sun gloves and cold weather gloves are available in finger coverage and fingerless models. Most of these have some grip feature to help hold the fish. Those gloves made with neoprene seem to do the least damage to a fish's coating. Although gloves are accepted practice, nearly everyone agrees that wet, uncovered hands constitute the least impactful way to handle a landed fish.

On the towel subject, the window for success for that fish handling technique is a narrow one. The towel must be clean, nonabrasive, and sopping wet to protect the fish. With a lot of usage requirements, towels may not be the best option.

Using your hand, or glove, or towel on a landed fish, remove the hook and return the fish to the water with some haste. Health outcomes worsen as each minute elapses.

BAROTRAUMA

For bass caught deeper than 28 feet, a caveat exists to the plan for quick release. This seldom applies to largemouth bass, as they prefer shallow waters most of the year. It would be more often applicable to spots, smallmouth, and stripers. In a similar way to a scuba diver getting the bends from ascending too quickly, fish rapidly brought to the surface from below 28 feet can suffer barotrauma.

Atmospheric pressure essentially doubles every 30 feet underwater. At 30 feet, water pressure rises to two atmospheres. At 60 feet underwater, pressure increases to three atmospheres. The fight between an angler and a hooked fish may yield quick changes in the depth at which the fish is swimming. Rapid decompression has physical impacts on a fish.

The physical signs of barotrauma are evident to even an imperceptive angler. A common manifestation of barotrauma is bulging eyes. Worse than eyes ballooning, a fish's stomach can distend, even to the point of it protruding from the fish's mouth. Expansion of the swim bladder contributes to both of these symptoms.

Depressurized swim bladders do not generally reset quickly enough for a bass to survive its new environment. Even if the fish is returned to the water, a few feet of water pressure is often insufficient to levelize its organs. A bass will attempt to descend, fighting against the enlarged swim bladder. Most run out of energy before achieving the necessary depth. A fish showing barotrauma symptoms subsequently released at the surface will likely perish.

Keeping the fish might be the best option. For those intent on releasing the creature, proper release of a bass with barotrauma is possible. However, it is complicated. Two methods are recommended, detachable weights and a syringe.

Barotraumatized fish can be returned with the aid of some equipment. The least invasive method of releasing a fish with barotrauma is to return it to the water with a detachable weight. The weight drags the fish down to a depth consistent with pressure equalization. Counting down to 30 feet, the angler unclips the weight to release the fish. This method requires some purpose-built equipment.

The other response is a bit more surgical. Using this method, an angler would insert a syringe needle into the fish's swim bladder to bleed off some of the excess air. Once the swim bladder is partially deflated, a barotraumatized fish could be returned safely to surface waters. Thankfully, barotrauma is not a frequent occurrence in large-mouth bass fishing. Yet, next-level anglers should be prepared to save the fish on these rare occasions.

SCENTS

All of this fish handling can have some implications for subsequent catches. Amines rubbed from the fish's slime coat stay on an angler's hands. These chemicals can be pungent. The slime coat is not the only scent exposure. Fish tissue contains a more aromatic amine called trimethylamine. Trimethylamine reacts to oxygen. The chemical reaction releases ammonia as fish tissues decay.

An angler handling a fish out of the water will retain the slime coat aroma. If unhooking takes a few minutes, anglers will likely add an ammonia smell on their hands. Once ammonia contacts human skin, it is not easy to rinse it away. Water alone does not clear the chemical.

Few anglers enjoy these smells. Moreover, the scents may impact future fishing results. Removing the scent is recommended. Thankfully. equipment on board a boat offers some potential relief. Stainless steel and soap are remedies.

Some live wells are constructed using stainless steel liners. Stainless steel has a chemical reaction with ammonia. That reaction changes the ammonia molecule and carries it away. An angler rubbing her hands on the sides of a stainless live well can discharge the ammonia smell.

While contact with stainless steel may be available, it is not a fool-proof method due to coatings, grades of material, and environmental considerations. Hand washing is the next step. Ammonia can be eliminated with soap, vinegar, lemon juice, or toothpaste. Most anglers do not have either kitchen essentials or toiletries on their boat, but some do carry a mild soap. If the discharge from washing with soap and water can be kept to a minimum, ammonia can be removed while on the water.

Removing the slime and ammonia can be as problematic to anglers as leaving it. Bass seem to be able to recognize soap fragrances, even trace amounts in terms of parts per million. It is hard to know whether soap or ammonia smells are more threatening to future bites. Relying on the presence of large quantities of water to dissipate the amine or the cleanser may not be a winning strategy.

The issue of scent gets even more complicated if a fish is injured. Injuries can come from body punctures, cuts, or something as simple as a bass flopping a few times on a boat deck. When injured, a bass will release a pheromone called schreckstoffen. The pheromone acts as a danger signal to other bass. In response to schreckstoffen in the water, bass will flee the area. Anglers dealing with amines and pheromones which are likely to impact future bites face some potentially difficult scent challenges.

Scent challenges are not limited to fish handling. Not only do fish recognize danger signals from fish secretions, but also they seem to have acquired a sensitivity to human smells. Bait companies have demonstrated that bass can learn the smell of sunscreen, bug spray, nicotine, and gasoline. The oils from these substances get on anglers' hands. From the hands, they are frequently transferred to lures.

Scents potentially offensive to bass are hard to avoid. It would be unusual for an angler to start out a morning without applying sunscreen. Moreover, summer evening fishing trips are far more comfortable with bug spray applied to the neck and ankles. Most people use their hands to apply these lotions, and it is hard to break the habit of applying protection lake or riverside.

Anglers are far more effective when they are able to mask offending scents. Ammonia-scented fingers could thwart future bites. Soap-rinsed hands could be no better. Sunscreen or bug spray residue on a lure could act as a fish repellant. To avoid this problem, some companies make a hand wash specifically for anglers.

Since it is hard for an angler to remain scent-free, masking the troubling scents with scents that fish do like offers a potential salve. Crayfish, worm, and shad are attractive flavors to bass. Such artificial scents applied to bass baits have become an accepted fishing practice. Some plastic baits are impregnated with smells, and liquid sprays and gels are readily available. Artificial scents are effective, and they are widely used.

Although the liquid scents are designed to be applied to bait, those products can also be applied as a hand rinse. Artificial scents can be used to cover the ammonia, soap, and other human smells. Anglers may not find the smell an improvement over ammonia, but scent-covered hands will not prove an impediment to subsequent fishing. Blocking bad scents and using favorable ones will turn your nibbles into bites.

CHAPTER 10
Professionalism:
The conduct, aims, or qualities that characterize or mark a professional person. [1]

Bass fishing has been a long-standing youth sport. As with other athletic endeavors, kids are specializing in bass fishing at early ages. The pursuit of a college scholarship is becoming a greater possibility. As with all sports, a small number of collegians turn professional. For those that wish to make bass fishing a career, three prominent tours provide a forum.

SPECIALIZATION

Once a means of sustenance, then a form of recreation, fishing is evolving into a competitive sport. In all athletic endeavors, this generation of kids has been encouraged to specialize in a sport at an early age. As early as age seven, athletic kids are recruited for traveling soccer teams and those with developed eye-hand coordination start playing baseball year-round. Malcom Gladwell's observation that it takes about 10,000 hours of practice to master the fundamentals of a sport is now generally accepted doctrine.[2] Other studies suggest that athletic training for more than 16 hours per week becomes counterproductive. Those two figures make for easy math. Take 10,000 hours and divide by 16 hours per week. The

---

1 Retrieved November 7, 2020, from https://www.merriam-webster.com/dictionary /professionalism.
2 Gladwell, Malcolm. *Outliers*. Little, Brown & Company, 2008.

mathematical product is that it takes 12 years to make a potential professional athlete, and one can turn pro around the age of 20 in many sports.

Fishing has a long history of appealing to children. In 2019, one quarter of all anglers were between the ages of six and 12. Being a kid-friendly endeavor has many positives. Most of the professional anglers in this book reveal meaningful fishing experiences in their childhood years. Destin DeMarion was lakeside with his grandfather at age three. Pam Martin-Wells was outfishing her parents and siblings at age seven. Brandon Palaniuk connected with his mentor at age nine. A relationship between early fishing success and ultimate next-level angling does seem to exist.

Striking a balance between formative fishing experiences and an advancement path appears to be difficult. Some kids are concentrating their athletic efforts on the sport of fishing. As an example of the investment being made in competition for kids, 108 youths competed in the Junior National Championship last year. At least two junior tours have sprouted up, bringing competitive situations and national travel to anglers as young as second grade. As an indication that specialization in this sport may be premature at such ages, most of the junior anglers are too young to be eligible for fishing licenses.

Pressures continue into high school. Fishing has become a cut sport in many high schools as the competitive bass fishing has become more mainstream. For a single West Texas high school tournament last year, 178 teams (356 kids) launched boats on Lake Whitney last year.

As with other sports where intense competition begins before middle school, risks of burnout and injury are high. According to an American Medical Society for Sports Medicine study, 12 percent of kids specialize in a sport before age six. Over 70 percent of kids specialize before age 11.[3]

Specialization is the number one cause of overtraining and its resultant psychological and physical maladies. Injury rates range from

---

3   DeFiori, John et. al. "Overuse injuries and burnout in youth sports." *British Journal of Sports Medicine.* Volume 48. Issue 4. 2013.

Carter Carriere. *Photo by Tyler Carriere.*

150 percent of average to 350 percent of average for young sports specialists. Anglers generally do not blow out knees or suffer concussions. However, for those wanting to discount the likelihood of fishing injuries, you may want to reconsider. Common training-related fishing injuries include carpal tunnel syndrome and angler's elbow. Carpal tunnel syndrome is often caused by repetitive motion, and it leads to arthritis later in life. Angler's elbow is something like tennis elbow. However, it impacts ligaments on the outside of the joint. It is a chronic injury that requires a surgical fix in extreme cases.

Competitive training has increased, and with it comes stressors. Bass fishing is at something of a crossroads in terms of youth participation. Early exposure often leads to passion for a lifetime sport, but early specialization risks burnout and injury. Something seems misaligned. Evidence shows a steep drop-off in fishing participation by teenagers. Making a recreational outlet into a constant competition may be a contributing cause.

COLLEGE

Although elite-level training before puberty has clear health risks, competitive bass fishing opens promising avenues to college-aged young adults. After wrestling for years to balance coursework loads with the travel requirements of bass fishing, colleges seem to have found a compromise. Colleges now treat bass anglers like other student athletes.

Team fishing is getting big on the college level. Last year, 116 schools competed, and a weekly top 25 ranking was produced, similar to that of college football. In another similarity to college football, schools are beginning to compete on the basis of facilities. Lake access and boat storage are among the recruiting tools. In a stark difference from revenue sports, however, small schools are well represented in the Top 25. Bryan College finished 2020 as the top-rated team in one fishing series and the second-rated team in another.

Some college sports have off-season training, like spring football or fall baseball. College fishing has a prominent late-season training event. The annual summer bass fishing camp has become a mecca for college anglers. The camp has 250 attendees, and it sells out within days once registration opens. The event has been held at Murray State each of the last few years, and each college angler is encouraged to have a coach accompany them to the series of seminars. Beyond angling itself, the camp highlights career opportunities in marine mechanics and fishing multimedia.

Little scholarship money is available for student angler athletes. Bethel University was the first school to offer bass fishing scholarships, and now about a dozen schools offer some funding. Three collegiate fishing tours have corporate sponsors, and some of that money defrays travel and equipment costs absorbed by students.

Pam Martin-Wells coaching Emmanuel College. *Photo by Stephen Wells.*

Pam Martin-Wells coaches 26 student anglers competing on the college circuit. Emmanuel College fields teams in both the Bassmaster College Series and the FLW College Fishing League. After teaching strategy, Martin-Wells directs practice from the shore of Lake Hartwell. When her team is prepared, Martin-Wells dispatches the 24 men and two women to regional events. The college participates in tournaments as far as 500 miles away from Franklin Springs, Georgia. Transportation is no small concern, as the young drivers must pull their own boats. Pam must worry about aspects such as driving. Her team sees her as a parental figure such that she received Mother's Day cards from the kids last year. With a family-oriented group and a legendary-angler-turned-coach, Emmanuel College is on its way to cracking the top 25 rankings. These student athletes are experiencing what life is like for professional anglers.

WOMEN'S TOURS

Women have competed in professional bass fishing for more than a decade. The Women's Bassmaster Tour (WBT) had several successful seasons beginning in 2006. Dianna Clark won the first women's Angler of the Year award that year. Two years later, Kim Bain-Moore was the first woman to get an invitation to the sport of fishing's biggest event, the Bassmaster Classic.

Despite several success stories, few women have advanced to compete regularly at the sport's top events. Successes have been celebrated. However, those celebrations have been few.

To the credit of the women anglers, most point out that the bass themselves cannot tell the difference between lures cast by those with X or Y chromosomes. This sort of statement implies that the women believe that they have an equal chance on the water. While the competitive opportunity may be fair, some signs of gender bias remain. For example, an Arkansas fishing tour still today calls itself "Mr. Bass."

Breakthroughs for women have been few, and the WBT folded in 2010. A year later, however, it was replaced by the Lady Bass Anglers Association (LBAA). Now in its 10th season, the LBAA maintains a four-tournament schedule. The tour recruits new female anglers, and it makes it easy for non-boaters to participate. You will never guess who was the most recent Angler of the Year. Yep, it's Pam Martin-Wells.

Opportunities continue to emerge for women to qualify for the more high-profile fishing tours. However, it is not an easy task. Sponsorship dollars are hard to attract, and a community of female anglers is lacking. Trait Zaldain is the most recent woman to pursue this path.

HIGHEST ECHELON

Reaching the professional level in bass fishing requires qualifying for one of two leagues: Bassmaster or Major League Fishing (MLF). Bassmaster has been the gold standard in the industry for decades. The Bass Anglers Sportsman Society held its first tournament in 1967, and it launched the precursor to today's Bassmaster Elite series in 1989. Thirty years later, a group of accomplished anglers broke off from Bassmaster to establish the MLF tour. Even more recently, Major League Fishing merged with Fishing League Worldwide (FLW), combining the top-level tour with a sizable feeder system. A few anglers transition from one league to another, but in general, the leagues are not on friendly terms. Each has a separate path for qualification.

Bassmaster's top tour is the Bassmaster Elite series. The Elite series has a signature tournament, the Bassmaster Classic. It is the biggest bass fishing event in the world. To non-anglers, the Classic would be explained as the sport's singular, high-profile event. I would compare it to the Indianapolis 500 in open-wheel motorsports.

Bassmaster's format is to weigh the five largest fish from each angler at the end of each tournament day. Elite tournaments begin with about 85 preselected anglers. Over half of the field is cut after the first two days, and only the Top 10 anglers fish on the final day.

Qualifying for the Elite tour is a difficult and expensive task. Bassmaster hosts two regional leagues, the Central and the Northern. Each of these leagues holds four open tournaments within their region. Any angler can compete in the Opens. The $1,500 entry fee wards off the unserious. Anglers are scored according the weight of the bass caught in each event. Order of finish in each event is tabulated. For those who participate in multiple Open events, the combined scores for all of the events are accumulated. The top five finishers in each region qualify for the next Elite tour.

Qualifying for the Elite tour is highly competitive. Margins of victory are measured in singular ounces. Once qualified, staying Elite is equally hard. About 15 percent annual turnover is normal for the tour.

Major League Fishing is a tournament series created by a group of professional anglers who split off from Bassmaster. One of the original motivations for MLF was to promote individual athletes. To that end, MLF takes breaks from fishing every 2.5 hours for periods of media access. While print and internet media-friendly, they are also television-friendly. The Outdoor Network broadcasts tournaments. MLF's format is to measure the weight of any qualifying fish caught by each angler. The number of fish caught is not capped. An angler could win a MLF tournament by catching the most one-pound and larger fish, not necessarily the biggest.

The MLF tour is now fed anglers by FLW. FLW, for most of its history, has been a grassroots fishing organization. Part of its grassroots identity, many FLW tournaments do not charge entry fees. Attracting anglers for whom costs are prohibitive, the tour has broadened participation in the sport. Tournaments can be quite crowded, with as many as 200 registrants, although that quantity of anglers is seldom on the water at the same time.

The entry level is the Bass Fishing League (BFL), and BFL has an annual championship called the All-American Championship. Graduates from BFL matriculate to the FLW tour. There are 32 separate FLW series. Those achieving success in one of the FLW series move up to the FLW Pro tour. Some fungibility exists between the FLW and the FLW Pro tours. They hold several combined events. Winners at the FLW Pro level ascend to the MLF events. It can take several years for a rising angler to reach the top tour.

For those with high-level skills who can afford the entry fee, the Bassmaster Opens are the quickest way to the top of the profession.

For those needing a little skill-sharpening and those for whom fees are a hurdle, MLF offers a longer but still-productive route. Format differences make it difficult for anglers to cross over between MLF and Bassmaster.

CHAPTER II

Focus:

A state or condition permitting clear perception or understanding.[1]

In Daniel Kahneman's book *Thinking Fast and Slow*,[2] the author describes two consecutive human responses to a problem. An instinctual response is followed by a logical response. Christiana Bradley has sensory skills, which makes her instinctual. In addition, she has the mind of an IT analyst (her day job), giving her the ability to interpret complex inputs. Instinctual and logical, Christiana Bradley fishes fast and slow.

Christiana grew up on the east slopes of the Shenandoah Mountains a bit more than an hour from the headwaters of the Rappahannock River. While only 40 miles from Washington D.C., the area near Fredericksburg, Virginia is at the edge of the wilderness. South of town, the Massaponax Creek flows through Ruffins Pond and into the river. The creek is curvy and shallow. It looks like a mountain stream. The channel is studded with large rocks that look beige when they mound above the water. The clear water flows gently but relentlessly over the cobble.

In the relatively tight quarters of the creek between shoreline grasses and overhanging trees, Christiana hung her head over the side of the canoe. In her field of vision from a foot above the water, she was seeing life. She watched shad thrash up the creek. She discovered black tadpoles

---

1   Retrieved November 7, 2020, from https://www.merriam-webster.com/dictionary/focus.
2   Kahneman, Daniel. *Thinking Fast and Slow*. Farrar, Straus & Giroux. 2011.

waving their spotted tail blades. Her line of sight was occasionally disrupted by a water strider skating across the surface.

From the back of the canoe, her brother Gary realized something. He was casting to what he thought to be prospective fishing spots while Christiana was actually seeing the forage. With her head turned partially to the side, he could see her eyes tracking the underwater activity. She would drop a finger into the water, seeming to point the way to the fish.

If a person can be astounded, but not surprised, that was Gary's reaction. For years, he knew Christiana as his "secret weapon." He referred to her as such. She was instinctually good at sports. She was one of those people who could see the spin on a ball. Not only did she have a sense for ball games, she was also the kind of girl who when she punched you, it actually hurt. Her gifts seemed God-given and natural.

As the canoe drifted downstream, Gary unscrewed the catch securing the crank on his reel. He reversed the crank, outfitting it to suit his left-handed sister. He had a moment of reluctance in handing over his prized St. Croix rod and reel, but he ultimately felt compelled to do so. He offered her the fishing pole. She accepted, and without a moment's hesitation she cast. The lure flew straight to where she knew a fish would be suspending. Upon landing in the water, the bait disappeared. The largemouth bass she reeled aboard would be the first of many.

Encouraged by her first catch, she redoubled her efforts. As Gary steered the boat over a shallow section of the creek, Christiana tracked the scattering minnows. Farther on, she identified bugs moving among tall spindles of grass. She heard chirps from tiny frogs before seeing them begin leaping. Seeing wildlife is Christiana's brain thinking fast.

While she watched, she balanced the rod on her lap. Christiana got unusually quiet. She pulled her long brown hair back into a ponytail, and she took a moment to think slow. She squinted her brown eyes, lowered her head, and "put the puzzle together." After a few minutes Gary started losing patience, and she turned and started to verbalize. She knew why the fish were where they were.

Gary offered some coaching. He told her that finding the fish was one thing but that catching them was another. Could she cast well enough? Did she have the right lure? Can she "fish her fish?" She absorbed the advice and pinpointed her next cast. Gary wondered if he would ever get his rod back.

Christiana Bradley in a moment of meditation while reconfiguring her lure. *Photo by James Overstreet; originally published in Outdoorshooter .com*

SIGHT FISHING

In most places during the early spring, bass can be targeted by sight. Just as Christiana could look through the water to view shad and tadpoles, the same can be done for bass. A common technique for spring fishing is to look over the shallows from a perch atop one's boat. When the water is crystal clear, and the fish can be viewed directly. Under stained and silty water conditions, which are more common in the spring, the bass appear as the blue or green football shapes above a light-colored bottom. With respect for sun angle and a few pieces of gear, next-level anglers can visually target their quarry.

To state the obvious, seeing the fish is what makes sight fishing. Sun angle plays an important part. Looking into the sun narrows one's vision to a squint. The sun forward of the angler also casts a glare on the water that can be as blinding as the sunlight itself. Sight fishing is difficult with a narrow field of vision.

Visibility improves if the sun is positioned behind the angler. However, that is not without nuance. The angler has to take care not to reveal her presence with a long shadow. With sun intensity and sun angle both factoring into success, sight fishing often picks up a few hours into the fishing day.

Sight fishing is possible with the naked eye, but equipment aids the effort. Polarized eyewear sharpens the image. Not only is polarization useful, some sunglass tints improve visual acuity. Tints eliminate spectra of sunlight reflecting from the water. While other shades have application, amber-tinted lenses are optimal for fishing under most conditions.

Working shallow water in bright conditions, visibility is high for both the angler and the fish. Sight-fishing success improves with light tackle. Disappearing line is a must. So, Christiana recommends threading a spinning rod with either fluorocarbon line or a fluorocarbon leader. A six-pound test is plenty strong enough, in most situations, as anglers generally are not contending with either cover or vegetation when sight fishing.

Along with some specialized gear, variations from a typical bass presentation are recommended for sight fishing. Reaction strikes are to be avoided. Typically, a bass might strike a lure in response to a bait splashing into the water just above its head. In shallow, clear conditions if it does not attack an intrusive lure, the fish will flee. "Hitting a bass on the head" with a lure placement will likely result in a sight-fishing opportunity lost.

To prevent the possible flight, the recommended sight-fishing technique is to present a lure parallel to the fish. Christiana will cast a brightly colored tube several yards ahead and a few feet to the side of the visible animal. When Christiana retrieves the lure, the parallel motion triggers a natural predatory response from the bass.

Although it is a conditioned response, this reaction may not occur during the first retrieve. It may take several passes to activate the fish. In addition, the fish may not ingest the lure on its first attack. Bass may bump or nip the tube. Second-chance casts to a spot where bass have engaged a passing lure are often effective. The odds of success increase if subsequent passes deploy different-colored lures. While parallel passes catch roaming bass, sight-fishing lures and methods change drastically if a fish is suspending above a spawning bed.

CHASING THE SPAWN

Christiana has been sight fishing since her teenage years, and she has refined her technique. She has become one of the best sight anglers in the world, and she tries to use that advantage as much as conditions allow. Sight fishing works best during the spawning season. The trick for a sight-fishing specialist is to make the spawning season last a long time.

In the spring, species of fish take turns moving into shallow water, fanning nests, and laying eggs. Each fish species has something of a biological clock that tells them when to spawn. That clock is most sensitive to water temperature and to some extent moon phase. As a testament to grand design, for the most part, freshwater species do not all spawn at the same time. The sequence of consecutive spawns lasts as long as three months in any given region. Anglers who excel at sight fishing can chase the spawn and extend the shallow-water fishing season.

Largemouth bass are one of the first species to spawn each spring. Bass move into the shallows when water temperatures rise into the 50s for the first time. For anglers lacking a thermometer, this coincides with dogwood trees blooming and birds of prey preparing nests. Male bass swim into one- to three-foot depths in areas with silt or pea gravel bottoms. Male bass fan a nest which, when finished, can be as small as a frisbee or as large as a car tire. Moving the rock and silt often leaves scrapes on the body of a fish. Blood striping up and down fins is not unusual.

As the males are carving the beds, the females, the larger of the species, suspend offshore. Females are most often found scattered in four to seven feet of water, and they tend to congregate on a path between deeper haunts and the pending nests. When the work on the nest is completed, which can take more than a week, the males usher females into the prepared spaces. There, females deposit their eggs, sometimes in multiple nests, over the course of one to two days. Once they drop their eggs, the females retreat to the nearest cover. Males silt the eggs and suspend near the nest to guard it. Hatchlings will emerge in two to five days. At that point, the large males return to the depths.

For anglers, the spawn offers some of the best opportunities to sight a big fish. The largest bass spawn first. No one seems to know the precise reason. However, one speculation is that their larger body mass responds more quickly to the rising water temperature. Suspending and retreating females can be successfully located and subsequently targeted with crankbaits and spinner baits.

One of the most exciting times of the bass spawn happens when the fish are on their nests. Dark shadows are visible over the white-bottomed enclaves of exposed sand, shells, or pea gravel. Catching these nesting bass necessitates a willingness by the angler to irritate the fish. Bass are not feeding. However, they do not react favorably to an intruder in their nest, and their mouth is their weapon.

Soft plastic baits drawn along the bottom and dropped into the nest often provoke the fish. The size of the lure relative to the fish guides the reaction. Once an artificial lizard or crawfish or creature bait enters their nest, bass will push out smaller lures. For larger presentations, bass will suck up the intruder and swim it away. Those that swim it out can be hooked.

A second method of targeting bedding bass is to understand that bluegill prey on bass eggs and hatchlings. Bass know this tendency. A bluegill crankbait lingering over a nest will often elicit a defensive strike, especially from a male guarding the fertilized eggs.

The bass spawn is not the only early-season opportunity. Crappie will spawn when water temperatures rise to the mid–50-degree level. This temperature change could be days after the bass begin to spawn, or it could take a little longer. To the extent that their timing overlaps, crappie spawn in deeper water, generally in five- to 10-foot depths. On their way out of the shallows, bass may cross over the crappie beds. That may provide another opportunity for anglers. Deep-diving baits, which simulate crappie, may pick up a few predators feeding on the spawning crappie.

When the crappie complete their reproductive process, other species emerge. Carp and gar spawn about the same time. Longnose gar is a southeast regional fish. Gar move to their spawning beds when water temperatures reach the high 60s. Wholly different from crappie, gar spawn in water so shallow that their backs can stick out of the water. To find this shallow habitat, gar swim far up creeks or, in the alternative, far into the shallow corners of lake pockets. Feeding on gar is a high-risk activity for bass, as gar eat bass just as bass consume gar. Bass do have an advantage in the spring. The spawn distracts and subsequently exhausts the gar, giving bass some opportunities to feed. Like the bass spawn, the gar spawn is a visible one to anglers.

Seeing the gar spawn means knowing where to find bass. Bass will return to the shallow depths, occupying ambush spots near the escape routes from the gar spawning areas. For anglers, starting lures from the gar spawning beds and working them out to the waiting bass is often a successful strategy. Stick baits work well to emulate the gar.

Spawning season is not yet over when the gar complete reproduction. Bluegill begin to spawn when the water temperature exceeds 70 degrees. Like the gar, bluegill will spawn in as little as one foot of water. Like bass, bluegill carve nests for their eggs.

Bluegill are dainty fish. Their nests are near softball size, and they are often clustered such that the grouping looks like a honeycomb from a short distance. Their preferred nesting habitat is often found on less-steep shorelines often near development like rock beaches and roads. If these gravel areas are near some offshore cover, like a stump or a lay-down, you will likely find bluegill. Fish in this species can spend their entire lives within a small radius.

During their spawn, bluegill tuck into the shoreline and pair. Females deposit their eggs and leave, while males guard the nest for several days. Bass cruise near the spawning areas. They poach the nests, and they try to chase down bluegill coming and going to the mating areas. Bass anglers have several advantages during the bluegill spawn. They know where the bass will be in proximity to the bluegill nests. They know which direction the bluegill would likely be traveling, and they know the appearance of the prey. The largest bass Christiana has caught came proximate to bluegill beds.

In the southern states, the first spawn can begin as early as February. Spawning often continues until April or May. The spawning season begins as late as April in the northern states, and it may span into June. As an example from the northern tier, the Minnesota bass fishing season often starts in late May to protect the fish during the bulk of their mating season. An angler interested in optimizing the spawn could begin in the South and move progressively north fishing the same patterns for as long as four months. Shallow-water experts such as Christiana Bradley make this trek.

TEXAS RIGGED CRAWS

For fishing shallow-water cover, few lures outperform a Texas-rigged crawfish. Bass cannot resist an opportunity to feed on their favorite delicacy. Christiana knows how to fish this lure. She understands its range, its action, and its subtleties. Her fishing day will include a heavy dose of this high-confidence bait.

Texas-rigging requires three components, a bullet weight, a hook, and a soft plastic bait. A bullet weight looks like it sounds. The weight has the shape of a projectile, and it has a hollow channel from its point to its base where a fishing line can be fed through. Bullet weights come in several metals, but tungsten is growing in popularity due to its size-to-weight ratio. Tungsten is a heavier metal, so a ¼ ounce tungsten bullet is smaller than a ¼ ounce lead bullet weight. The weight is threaded up a fishing line, bullet point first. Once through the weight, the line is tied through a worm hook. After the hook is secured to the line, a soft plastic bait is threaded onto the hook. A pinch of the plastic rear fin of the craw is run through the hook barb and worked up the hook shank to the eye. The barb of the hook is then run back through the plastic near the head of the craw and "hidden" inside of it.

Hook sizes rage from 1/0 to 10/0. Anglers commonly refer to these as one gap to 10 gap hooks. Most anglers use a two gap or a three gap for Texas-rigging. Hooks also have different shapes, those being straight, offset, and Extra Wide Gap (EWG)—a hook which is both offset and curved. Different hook shapes work better in combination with different soft plastics. Crawfish plastics work best on straight hooks. Beyond gaps and offsets, hooks also have color choices. Red hooks are preferred for shallow-water sight fishing. The red color spectrum disappears first as light is filtered from water as depth increases.

The plastic element of a Texas rig can be a worm, a creature, a lizard, or a crawfish. Christiana says crawfish is the way to go. This decision drives a few of the rig specifications. Crawfish have more action when fished with light weights. Christiana suggests a weight no larger than 5/16 ounce for a Texas-rigged plastic craw.

Texas-Rigged Crawfish. *Photo by Joe Kinnison.*

Color choices are limitless for plastic baits, but Christiana focuses on a few universal colors. She believes that green pumpkin, june bug, and watermelon red are the only colors that a shallow-water angler needs to be successful. These color choices have the most natural appearance.

Just as the colors can be simplified, so can the action and size of the bait. "Flappy-style" crawfish baits have flat paddles in the place of pincers. The paddles are oversized relative to the body of the crawfish. These pincers are more evident to the bass, and they create more vibration in the lure. With better visibility and better action, deviating from flappy style is unnecessary. As for size, Christiana carries only two of the many crawfish lure sizes, and they are preloaded on separate poles when she begins her fishing day.

Gear for Texas-rigged craws is sight-fishing gear. Either a baitcaster or a spincaster reel will work for this lure. A medium-action rod works best, and fluorocarbon line is the choice for shallow or clear water. Of these elements, the line is the most important. The 12-pound test or lighter is the best choice, and the six-pound test is optimal.

With a nimble rod, a light line, and a light lure, a Texas-rigged crawfish can be cast with precision. Presentation is important for this lure, as it tends to be ineffective if it is dragged over limbs or other underwater obstructions lifting it above the bottom. Few crawfish fly up off the surface in reality. Seeing a crawfish in a Superman posture clues the bass to a problem. While it is great around laydowns, over-hangs, and grasses, a Texas-rigged craw should be used sparingly around rocks and riprap. The lure, though weedless, is susceptible to wedging itself under edges and snagging.

If the Texas-rigged craw does not prompt a bite on the fall, it should maintain bottom contact while being retrieved to the boat (no flying crawfish). Christiana keeps her rod tip pointed downward with the last eyelet just above the water surface. She reels slowly and steadily, stopping when she feels resistance. Christiana reports that biofeedback on bottom contour is available using this retrieve, and she believes that information on ridges, rocks, and shell beds is critical to ultimately locating the bass.

Most anglers use a Texas-rigged craw to explore the edges of a known structure. A usual approach would be to make several casts to parts of a fallen tree or several casts along a stand of pond weed. Beyond these traditional techniques, Christiana will use the lure as a search bait. She will throw it on edges of shallow flats. Not only will she probe new areas with the Texas rig, she will also employ the bait as a cleanup tool to capture stragglers in an area where she has already caught several fish. Whether saturating structure, searching for fish, or hooking the less-aggressive members of a school, she finds ample applications for a Texas-rigged crawfish on Lake Lewis Smith.

LAKE LEWIS SMITH

Lake Lewis Smith is a W-shaped lake of thin channels. In about 15 square miles of area, the lake has over 500 miles of shoreline. Hydrologically, it is not a big lake, holding only 20,000 acres of water, but do not let the low volume fool you. Large sections of the lake are more than 100 feet deep. Its maximum depth is 260 feet.

The original purpose of the lake was to support regular barge service for coal export. Parts of the lake look like they flooded the coal mine. Steep rock faces graduate into the water like terrace farms. Above the water, stone layers of flaky white and gray edge several areas near the dam.

Lake Smith Pier. *Photo by Christiana Bradley.*

The dam was the highest earthen dam in the nation when it was built. Lake construction started in 1957. It was completed in 1961. It took four years to move enough rock and soil to block the Sipsey tributary to the Black Warrior River.

Although not its original purpose, the dam does have a power plant. Testament to the dam's power generation function being secondary, Alabama Power only opens the spillways to offset peak power loads in the heat of the summer. It is unusual for a utility to use hydropower only when other power-generation sources have been exhausted.

With its great depths and rocky bottom, Lake Lewis Smith has the clearest water of any lake in Alabama. While clear end to end, the west side of the lake has more pristine water than the east side. Rocky creeks feed naturally filtered water to the west side. The east side gets some agricultural runoff, and it has an active park and marina, which stirs up sediment. Boaters on the west side frequently report visibility down beyond 20 feet.

When spring rains mix with the normally clear creeks, Christiana Bradley engages largemouths. On Lake Smith, the realm of the largemouths is mostly limited to the creeks. They swim to upstream cover for spawning. Otherwise, they dwell in the creek mouths. The reason for the limited range is that largemouth bass are not the apex predators in this lake.

Other species of bass are the top of the Lake Smith food chain. State record fish for both spotted bass and striped bass were caught on this lake. Alabama-strain is the largest strain in the spotted bass species. For over 30 years, the lake held the world record for a spotted bass caught on rod and reel. The eight-pound, 15-ounce whopper was only recently topped.

With all of those years atop the record charts, the lake is promoted as an Alabama Bass Tour stop for spotted bass. Spotted bass are smaller than their largemouth cousins. An average-sized spotted bass is about two pounds. Despite their diminutive size, the fish are coveted for their reputation as fierce fighters. The fish dive deep when hooked, and they are particularly adept at dragging fishing line under rocks and trees.

The fighting spots are hard to distinguish visually from the largemouth variety. They tend to be comparatively slender, and they have slightly more prominent black markings. These subtleties can be hard to discern. The more decisive physical difference is the mouth. The inside corners of the mouth of a spotted bass hinge forward of the fish's eye socket. The mouth of a largemouth will extend farther inward.

While appearance is similar, spotted bass have a habitat distinct from that of largemouths. Spots populate the deep channels. They suspend at 20- to 80-foot depths, and they school in large numbers. Spotted bass prefer current. They tend to thrive in rivers and lakes with flows. Lake Smith does not have much current, but the depths must suit the fish. For spots, anglers usually target offshore rock piles and river channel edges.

Given the small size of the fish and their propensity for clear water in which visibility is high, light tackle is often used to target spotted bass. Lure presentations are deeper. Drop shots, jigging spoons, and swim baits are common approaches.

Due to differences in terrain and gear, on Lake Smith, anglers typically pursue one bass species to the exclusion of the other. With anglers tempted to concentrate on the feistier but smaller spotted bass, a good stringer of five fish here weighs between 10 and 15 pounds.

Christiana says to skip the two marinas near the dam if you are fishing for largemouth. Instead, launch at the Duncan Bridge Marina, which is a span of blue girders siting low atop concrete piers. For some reason, the bridge seems to fascinate visitors. It is one of the most photographed parts of the lake. The marina and bridge even inspired a local artist to paint a watercolor.

Starting a day at the Duncan Bridge Marina saves considerable time motoring on the lake. Unloading can be something of a trick. The lake level varies by about 15 feet over the course of a year, and the launch area gets a little tight at low pool. Once on the water, it is a relatively short run north to Devil's Branch, a long creek bed with depths averaging five feet. The next largemouth bass terrain farther north is the Butler Branch. That cove features two intersecting creeks and an island. The channels and ledges often hold suspending bass.

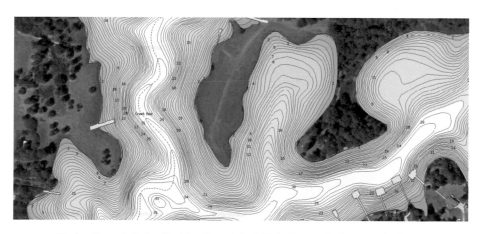

Butler Branch Lake Smith. *Copyright 2021 Garmin Ltd or its subsidiaries. All rights reserved. Used with permission.*

Locals give directions on this lake according to a spiderweb of surrounding county roads. It would not be unusual for someone to say something like "the fish are biting near County Road 3918." Using that same parlance, some suggest that visiting anglers targeting largemouth go uplake beyond County Road 292 and into the Coon Creek section. This area offers a number of mini points and bays. Largemouths favor the varied coastline.

The opportunity to fish clear creeks attracts Christiana to Lake Smith. Parts of the lake feel like the upper Rappahannock River of her youth. Yes, fishing is the prime attraction, but Christiana also likes to visit Jasper, Alabama. Jasper is the gateway town to the Duncan Bridge Marina. A few miles of Curry Highway connect the two. According to Christiana, Jasper is an angler-friendly town that "just gets it," in outfitting visitors to Lake Smith.

Starting from Birmingham, Alabama, take Interstate 22 northwest for 41 miles. Exit on State Road 269 and drive a few more miles to Jasper, which serves as one of the primary staging areas for lake trips. The whistle-stop town boasts a quaint Main Street backing to a railroad track.

Restaurants are the attraction in Jasper. Black Rock Bistro is one of the top restaurants in Alabama, according to *New York* magazine. It is open for lunch and weekend dinners. This Creole-inspired place might tempt you with Stuffed Catfish Pontchartrain. It is a little expensive for a fishing trip, but it is well worth it. Black Rock is not the only stop in town for foodies. Nearby Los Reyes has the best Mexican cuisine Christiana has ever tried.

While in town for a meal, stroll to the town square for some other memorable shops. At the end of Main Street sits a throwback men's haberdashery named Bernard's. Men are greeted at the door with coffee or Coke. The 125-year-old shop is filled with nostalgia and taxidermy. Anglers should not miss Pat's Archery and Outdoors for any last-minute gear needs.

While Jasper has restaurant and shop attractions, the best lodging options are on the shores of Lake Smith. Campsites and RV slabs are available near the Duncan Bridge Marina. The Duncan Bridge Resort Condos are a convenient low-rise near the boat launch, and a number of lakeside private homes and cabins are available for rent.

If you are ready to set out on the lake, try the following guide service. Fishing reports from Lake Smith have been great. Blueback herring were stocked in the lake. The stocking expanded the forage base, and bass sizes have exploded upward. The lake fishes well in all four seasons. It is noteworthy that good stringers have been reported in recent winters. Despite the improving bass girth, the lake is not overrun with anglers.

Lewis Smith Fishing Guide Service

Brent Crow's Guide Service   256-466-9965   brentcrow@bellsouth.net

DEVELOPING A SINGULAR TALENT

Some people do one thing really well. Such specialists thrive in many walks of life. Long driving champs have a niche in golf, for example. Some performers dance expressively, but neither act nor sing.

For those with an exceptional skill, finding opportunities to use that capability can become a challenge. Applications that make good use of that talent may be few. When an occasion to show off exceptional skill arises, paradigm-changing performances are either celebrated or, more often, treated with suspicion.

Optimizing a singular skill can be socially difficult. Victories can be discounted. Christiana wins again. Yawn. Alternatively, haters attempt to diminish specialists for cherry-picking events that fit their specialty. Other deniers highlight weaknesses in related disciplines. As in, "yeah but she cannot fish a swim bait" (She can. It's a hypothetical.), "so her dominance in craws is hollow." Those with pronounced, singular skills can be under constant pressure to broaden their abilities instead of exploiting their strengths.

Discouragement of a specialist can be overcome through working to build confidence. While true in most endeavors, confidence is a particularly crucial element in fishing. Many casts are likely necessary to yield a single bite. Confidence drives needed persistence.

With social pressures testing confidence, people with an uncommon talent thrive with a mentor. Someone who can provide a supportive environment enables a mentee to commit to her talent. A trusted voice gives permission to a mentee to use her abilities. With emotional support, a specialist is often motivated to excel.

Ideally, the mentor would be a coach—someone willing to reinforce the exemplary skill and to provide constructive feedback. A coach might arrange training to further increase the athlete's advantage or assist in the mental preparation for competition. Pushing someone to the edge of their special ability can motivate those with exemplary talents.

A mentor/mentee relationship may be its most impactful for those with a special skill. Yet, even those without a specialty depend on third-party advice. Every professional angler in this book has a mentor. This is not atypical for bass fishing. The sport has many oral traditions. It is not unusual for fishing skills to be translated from father to son and friend to friend. Bass fishing has an often-underestimated social element.

Most bass boats have seats for two anglers, one for the mentor and one for the mentee. That relationship need not be a static one. Anglers having mastered different techniques can help each other. For example, friendly swapping of information on color choices or scent flavors can reinforce one's fishing acumen.

Anglers can be successful by focusing on a standout technique. For those with a gift, impact can be maximized by selecting situations that best fit the skill set. Some fortitude is required, as social dynamics can be prickly. As such, optimizing a singular skill goes much better with the aid of a mentor or coach.

PAUSING

Thinking fast maximizes Christiana's strength in shallow-water sight fishing. Thinking slow has produced some of her best moments. Not long after winning a company fishing tournament, Christiana paused at the women's tour booth at the 2004 Bassmaster Classic. She ended up joining the tour and accessing the best fisheries in the country. On the tournament trail, she paused her fishing during one event to give her co-angler a chance to win a title. It was a moment of particular personal growth for her.

Recently, she put on hold her pursuit of becoming the first woman to qualify for the Elite tour. Christiana has a full-time job and an important role. Her employer enabled her to pursue a second career in fishing, sponsoring her effort. Fishing sponsors have proven elusive for many female anglers, so the financial support, which can near six figures, is material. Despite the support, four years of managing a weekday job and a series of professional fishing tour dates began to weigh heavy on the angler. Wanting to allocate some vacation time to family endeavors, she paused.

Gary and Christiana. *Selfie by Christiana.*

To recapture her passion for the sport, Christiana has reconnected with her brother and modified their previous fishing arrangement. Christiana is no longer the scout. Now they work together, cordially and competitively, as only siblings can, with some good-natured bickering involved. She arranges lake outings, and Gary hosts river outings. She slows him down, and he speeds her up. The relationship between adult siblings, who spent hours and hours fishing together as children, has evolved. It has a pleasant mix of fast and slow.

CHAPTER 12
Selection:
The act or process of selecting.[1]

The fishing industry is blessed with innovative gear. Over the past few decades, advancements in rod, reel, and line technologies have produced meaningful advantages for anglers. Modern equipment casts farther and reels smoother. Advanced fishing lines are more durable and less visible.

Technological advancement has not neglected fishing. However, by itself, leading-edge equipment is not guaranteed to catch more bass. Rather, having the right combination of equipment and using it under the optimal circumstances raises an angler to the next level.

RODS

Bass rods are distinguished by their length, action, and power. Other fishing disciplines use shorter and longer versions, but bass fishing rods range in length from six feet to 7½ feet. Shorter rods foster more precision. Longer rods improve casting distance, and they are most often used for flipping and pitching.

No matter the length, rods have similarities in construction. Graphite and fiberglass are the most utilized construction materials. The great majority of bass rods are composites, or combinations of both materials. Composite rod construction starts with a fiberglass blank. A blank is a bundle of glass strands. The strands are wrapped in a graphite mesh. The mesh is called a scrim. The scrim-wrapped blank is then coated in

---

1   Retrieved November 7, 2020, from https://www.merriam-webster.com/dictionary /selection.

resin, which glues the components together. Eyelets, called windings, are lashed on with thread. The rod is completed with a notch, which acts as a seat for a reel.

Rods are differentiated by action and power. Action identifies the point on the shaft at which the rod begins to bend. Action can range from extra fast to slow. With extra-fast-action rods, only the top third of the pole will flex. The top eyelet will deflect up to 30 degrees from the shaft. Sample one in a Bass Pro or Walmart store, and you will be amazed by how slight 30 degrees seems for a fishing rod. With little flex in the rod, the angler's response to a bite can be rapid. A high proportion of the movement of the rod translates to the hook. Although the speed at which a hook can be set is the fastest, the angler faces a trade-off when choosing an extra-fast-action rod. The stiff rod is likely to reduce casting distance.

At the opposite extreme action from extra fast is the appropriately named slow. The top two-thirds of a slow-action rod will bend, and the top eyelet on the rod tip will deflect as much as 90 degrees from the core. This flexibility greatly enhances casting distance, adding a whip effect to the cast. Yet, that distance comes at a cost. Due to the proclivity of the rod to bend, much more movement is required of the angler upon hook set. As such, this rod action is most useful for panfish and crappie where a lighter hookset could be an advantage. Professional bass anglers seem to embrace neither extreme of extra fast nor slow. They gravitate toward medium-action rods.

Different from action, power indicates the ability of the rod to lift weight. Power is measured by the amount of bend in a fishing pole when it supports a one-pound weight. Think of action as the point at which a rod starts bending and power as how much it will bend. A rod's power can be heavy, medium, light, or a combination of those three factors. A heavy rod will stay nearly straight when supporting a one-pound weight, while a light rod will adopt a severe bend under similar strain. Anglers discussing a rod's power talk about how fast a rod will "load." Load means how fast a hookset will translate to the fish. They also consider how much a rod will deflect when the line it controls encounters

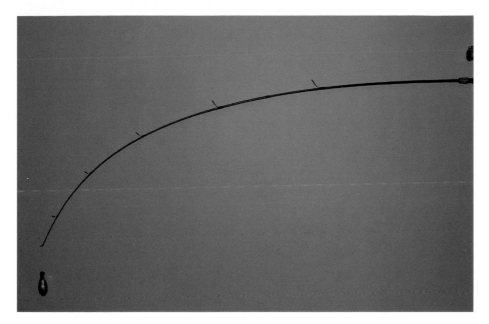

Inflection of a fast-action, medium-power rod. *Photo by Joe Kinnison.*

a hazard. Heavy-power rods load quickly, and they are not sensitive to impediments. A typical use case would be for fishing vegetation where a lure may have to be pulled through hang-ups. Light power loads slowly, and it is best suited for high-sensitivity or open-water situations.

Although action and power are the most distinguishing technical factors, a rod paired to support a particular reel is critical. A spinning rod will have a large eyelet closest to the reel base. The large eyelet accommodates a wide apex of line releasing from a spinning reel. Separate from a spinning rod, a casting rod has two notable features. Casting rods have a small first eyelet. In addition, they have a trigger-shaped protrusion below the reel base. This trigger aids the angler in keeping a grip on the rod while controlling a baitcasting spool with their thumb. Spinning reels can drag and tangle if paired with the small first eyelet of a casting rod. Baitcasting reels can be slippery on spinning rods lacking a trigger notch.

REELS

Bass fishing reels come in three varieties—spincasters, baitcasters, and spinning reels. Spincasters are functional reels for novice anglers. The

Zebco brand is virtually synonymous with spincasters. Few next-level anglers use spincasting reels on a regular basis. Baitcasting and spincasting reels each have application for bass anglers.

Baitcasting reels excel at casting distance and accuracy. Freshwater baitcasters use the low-profile varieties of the reel type. This design is short and sleek in comparison to the round baitcasters used by saltwater anglers. A low-profile baitcasting reel is designed so that the spool holding line is perpendicular to the shaft of the rod. This orientation allows fishing line to unwind from the spool straight down the rod. It eliminates friction during casting. Low friction can lead to improved casting distance. The spool positioning also enables easy control using an angler's thumb. An angler can apply pressure from a digit and slow or stop the line from unspooling at any moment. With thumb control, it is believed that baitcasting reels offer high casting accuracy.

As if improved casting performance was not enough, baitcasters also improve speed control. The reels are manufactured in a wide variety of gearings. For anglers who fish slowly or anglers employing lures requiring a slow presentation, baitcasters are available with a gear ratio as low as 5:1. The ratio indicates the number of turns of the spool for each turn of the crank, and 5:1 is really slow. Anglers using power techniques, burning and ripping lures, want a fast-moving bait. Gear ratios as high as 9:1 are available for that purpose. While either extreme is available, the majority of baitcasters have a gearing between 6.4:1 and 7.4:1.

Some anglers are able to pace their retrieve to contour the preset gear ratio. However, that ability is rare. More often, different gearings fit different fishing styles. Once a reel is constructed, the gear setting is not changeable.

Just as gearing cannot be reset, baitcaster cranks are also fixed. If the reel is constructed for a right-handed angler or a left-handed angler, it stays that way. This part of the design of the reel makes a baitcaster difficult to share.

Perhaps the biggest shortcoming of the reel is that baitcasters are susceptible to backlash. If an angler does not control the spool when the lure meets resistance, such as the water surface, the line on the spool winds back upon itself. It would not seem that a few backward turns of a spool could create a hellacious knot, but it can. Backlash can be difficult to untangle, taking several minutes to pick out the overlapping line. With a large consequence for mistakes, preventing backlash has a frustrating learning curve. To some degree, that learning never ends. Even next-level anglers face backlash problems on windy days. Wind can change the tension on a moving fishing line and that change, by itself, can result in the line knotting itself.

A baitcaster and a spinning reel. *Photo by Joe Kinnison.*

While baitcasters are the favored reels for bass fishing, some applications best fit spinning reels. A spinning reel orients the line spool so that the line un-spirals parallel to the rod. Spinning reels have a bail, which looks like a curved piece of wire with a tiny yo-yo body on the end. When the bail is in its up position, fishing line feeds freely from the reel through the eyelets of the rod. When the bail is in its down position, it holds the line in place and engages the reel handle for retrieve.

Spinning reels are traditionally fished from a position below the shaft of the rod. You might think of a spinning reel as being used upside down. Anglers control the free line by pinching it to the handle of a rod forward of the reel seat using the tip of their forefinger. The tip of the forefinger is a sensitive body part. With this connection between angler and line, spinning reels are believed to give anglers better feel for bites and bottom terrain. Given high sensitivity, spinning reels are the preferred reels for finesse fishing applications. Finesse applications include almost anything that employs a small lure or a soft plastic.

Separate from, though sometimes related to, finesse applications, spinning reels are often used in clear water. Spinning reels are designed to carry light line, usually 12-pound test or lower. The clearer the water, the easier bass can see. So, next-level anglers downsize to either leaders or full line packages with light line. Spinning reels are the right tool for clear-water, light-line presentations.

Spinning reels are also the correct choice for anglers who fish lakes and rivers replete with docks. Bass suspend under the decking of some docks. To catch them, lures must be delivered into the space below the planks and above the water. A lure would be skipped into that space using a nearly horizontal cast. Such casts are extremely difficult to accomplish with a baitcaster. The physics of the spool prevent it. However, spinning reels are ideally suited to flat casts. For the particular application of skip casting, the spinning reel is the optimal choice.

Use a baitcaster for casting and speed control. Utilize a spinning reel for finesse and horizontal presentations. Whichever reel you use, load it up with the proper line.

LINE

The number of fishing line options has expanded over recent years. Accompanying the innovation has been a significant increase in prices. Destin DeMarion sees fishing line as a significant cost item for anglers. For the cost, anglers pay for different line properties. Monofilament, fluorocarbon, and braid have distinct advantages.

Monofilament may be the longest-serving fishing line other than string. It may also be the cheapest. Monofilament is a single-strand nylon extrusion. The nylon stretches, helping anglers manage snags. Along with being stretchy, mono is buoyant. The line floats at the onset of a fishing day although it ultimately absorbs water through use. Floating line can slow the descent of some lures. Camouflage is another advantage of this type of fishing line. Nylon can be colored, and color selections that match the shade of the water can reduce visibility. For example, clear or blue mono can be used to hide the line in clear water. Green and gold mono can disappear in stained water.

Although it has positive features, such as stretch, buoyancy, and camouflage, the line also has a few bugs. Mono acquires a memory over time, keeping the turn from the reel. Those turns can prevent smooth casting, and they have a tendency to tighten and kink. Line memory can result in a bird's nest of twisted line. Along with growing more twisty over time, mono is also photosensitive. It breaks down after prolonged exposure to sunlight. The line gets brittle and loses some of its coloration.

While monofilament has traditionally been a full-spool line, fluorocarbon started out as leader material. The advantage of polyvinylidene fluoride is that it is completely invisible underwater. While stealthy, another feature of this substance is that fluorocarbon sinks. A sinking line can improve the performance of deep-diving baits and baits that perform best when they descend naturally. "Fluoro" does not stretch, making it sensitive and efficient in translating hooksets. It is a durable substance. In many ways fluoro has opposite properties of mono.

While it has many positive attributes, fluorocarbon has negatives. It is prone to knot failure. One of the most common knots in fishing is the clinch knot. Fluorocarbon must be treated gingerly when tying this knot. The line must be wetted for the knot to succeed. The knot must be tied slowly, and the tightening of the knot should be gradual to avoid friction. The knot can burn itself if tied with haste. Even with a delicate approach to knot tying, fluoro knots are unreliable after regular use. Anglers who use this line are best served to retie knots frequently. Beyond knot failure, the primary drawback to fluorocarbon is its price. The fishing line can cost twice as much per yard as mono.

Not cheap like monofilament or invisible like fluorocarbon, braid has other advantages. Braided line is about half the diameter of monofilament at the same test. It is thin and strong. The diameter comparison is not a linear relationship, but for example, a 0.014-inch diameter monofilament line will be a 12-pound test line. The same dimension braid line will have 50-pound test.

Like fluorocarbon, braid does not stretch. Unlike fluorocarbon, it also does not break. Those features help hooksets, but it also makes snags particularly difficult. Anglers will struggle to break the line. Braid does not acquire a memory over time. As such, it is one of the few types of fishing line that can be used for years and years on the same reel.

Visibility and wear are drawbacks for braid. Fish can see this line. That visibility limits its use. The line is also known to be hard on rod and reel parts. The line holds up, but the accompanying equipment may not.

Mono, fluorocarbon, and braid all have use cases. Matching the line to one's equipment and fishing style yields optimal results.

HOW MANY?

Professional anglers differ on the number of prepared rods requisite for a fishing outing. However, nearly everyone seems to agree that the figure should be in the double digits. Destin DeMarion seldom starts a fishing day with fewer than 10 rods on deck. Tyler Carriere will have about 20 stowed in his gunwales. Brandon Palaniuk seldom leaves the marina with fewer than 30 pre-strung combinations.

Tournament co-anglers are regularly limited to five rod-and-reel combinations. Just as with co-anglers, five is the recommended number of rods for a next-level angler. That quantity may seem high. It may also seem contrary to this book's frequent claims that equipment does not make the angler. However, rod-and-reel outfitting is the one area in which a broad set of basic equipment is recommended. Bass fishing techniques have differing technical requirements. To address different fishing situations, the five should include at least two spinning reels and at least two baitcasting reel assemblies.

The spinning reels are best deployed in two configurations. Lashed to a seven-foot light- to medium-power, fast-action rod, one spinning reel would be the first choice for soft plastics, including shaky heads. A second spinning reel set on a shorter (6'6") medium- to heavy-power rod would be the optimal setup for topwaters, jerkbaits, and Texas-rigged worms.

Varying gear ratios provide default baitcasting combinations with a few more wrinkles. A low gear ratio baitcasting reel paired with a seven-foot medium-power, medium-action rod would deliver good performance for crankbait fishing. A middling gear ratio baitcasting reel seated on a medium- to heavy-power, fast-action rod is the best delivery vehicle for jigs, spinner baits, and swim baits.

For the fifth basic rod-and-reel combination, a baitcaster on a long, stiff rod is a bass fishing necessity. A seven-foot, six-inch rod with heavy power and fast action is most suitable. These rods are utilized for flipping and pitching. Connected to a high gear ratio baitcaster, this setup is optimal for frogs, swim jigs, and chatterbaits.

To some degree, the number of riggings depends on the type of fishing expected. All five preparations may not be necessary if the body of water or the conditions disfavor a certain technique. For example, in a murky river after the spawn, it would be fine to leave the jerkbait combination at home. Replace that rod and reel with a second one suited to the lures you expect to throw.

The prescribed number of rod-and-reel combinations would rise above five if certain lure configurations are utilized. Drop shots and Carolina rigs take time to construct. The time to collect beads, swivels, and weights and tie those knots is best spent prior to the start of a fishing day. If your fishing plans anticipate either a drop shot or a Carolina rig, create a purpose-built pole with these rigs. Add it to your basic five.

Next-level anglers may not need the quantity of rod-and-reel combinations used by the pros. However, a minimum of five puts an angler in the best situation for delivery and retrieval of the myriad of bass fishing lures. A next-level angler would use more than five if complicated riggings are used or if frequent lure changes are contemplated. In this one particular case, the quantity of gear makes a difference.

CHAPTER 13
Originality:
Freshness of aspect, design, or style.[1]

Destin DeMarion was miserable. A relentless west wind was forming foamy peaks on Douglas Lake. The lake's shoals, normally a welcome site to anglers, looked like ice cubes surrendering to a fizzy drink. Above the surface, the gusts had cleared the usual mist from the surrounding Smoky Mountain hills. With shoals and hills succumbing, the lake felt unguarded.

Spray from the waves had the feel of frozen gains of sand as it hit against the exposed portion of Destin's bearded face. Sunglasses protected his eyes from the onslaught, but the tint gave both the lake and sky the same thunderstorm-green hue. Without the hood attachment, which was pulled tight to his forehead and tied to cover his chin, his glossy blue rain suit would not have been enough protection to enable him to tolerate the cold front. April days in Tennessee were not supposed to be this cold.

Weather was not his only challenge. His immediate future was out of his control. Destin had registered for the B.A.S.S. Southern Open as a co-angler. Co-anglers were relegated to the back seat of a two-person boat, away from the controls. He was at the mercy of a professional fisherman in the forward seat. Destin had met this pro a few hours ago at the dockside, and the fearsome weather inhibited getting acquainted. Given the pressure exerted by the ball of Joey Nania's foot on the black

---

1 Retrieved November 7, 2020, from https://www.merriam-webster.com/dictionary /originality.

plastic trolling motor petal, this fishing day would not be ending soon. Besides, Nania was slowly filling his live well. With a return trip to the marina out of the immediate picture, Destin was feeling his captivity.

He was also losing sensation in his toes. The boat's gray carpet-fuzz-covered deck was soaking up splashes, and Destin had left his waterproof footwear at home. His feet squished in his shoes as he pushed his leg hard against the red leather seat pedestal to steady himself from the waves. Turning his face downward to avoid a sudden outburst of sleet, he paused to stare longingly at the clear plastic tray filled with jigs, frogs, power worms, and lizards down on the deck.

His usual lures were in that tray, idle in a sleeve of his tackle box. At the tip of his rod was a Whip Em Rig. It was a variation of an Alabama rig, a newly legal, supposedly super lure. The rig had the appearance of uncovered parasol tines. Each tine had a different lure tied to the end of it. In the water, the baby crib mobile-looking contraption of a lure took on the appearance of a school of fish. Similar rigs were producing trophy results in other tournaments, but this one was new to Destin, and his confidence level was dropping with the temperature.

"Confidence," spoke a voice in his head. The sophic guidance counselor continued, "Fishing is about confidence." The remembered voice of his grandfather spurred him on. "Confidence comes from belief in something larger."

While the boat tracked slowly forward, Destin voiced a quiet petition. Following his amen, he squinted through the sleet to the two weatherproof screens mounted near Joey's feet. Through the drips tracing down the screens, he could see steep slopes on the lake bottom in yellow and black graphic relief. Joey had been scouring the sides of lake points with his own arsenal of lures. Destin extended his rod above his head to its full seven-foot length. He cast the umbrella rig. The company of artificial baits landed near the bank, and he began to retrieve the school of lures.

To the extent that prayers get answered immediately, his prayer landed in about five seconds. Destin's rod bowed, and the line extending from his baitcaster snapped taut. Destin gathered his stinging feet, sprung upright, and set the hook. The rig itself weighed several ounces, and with a fish hooked to one of the tines, he felt a heavy tow.

With the rod handle set against his chest, he labored to raise the bending rod tip. The apex of the rod rounded above his head. He pulled hard against the weight, drawing the fish toward the surface. As he made progress, Destin lowered the rod back toward the water, reeling as he did so to recover the line. He repeated the pumping technique. First, pull up. Second, recover line while tilting the rod back toward the water.

Ultimately, Destin guided the fish to the side of the boat. Joey scooped it aboard. It was only Destin's second fish of the day, but it was a big one. On a day when any fish was a good fish, his two-bass stringer placed Destin among the top amateurs in the tournament.

Destin's perseverance at Douglas Lake propelled him on his path to becoming a professional fisherman. Just as he did that day, each time he enters a Bassmaster Elite Tour tournament, he brings the memory of his departed grandfather with him.

FISHING BUDDY

Destin's mother returned to her parents' home when Destin was a few months short of his third birthday. His grandfather was getting ready to retire, and he had determined that he would be learning how to fish. Steve Slencak, a wispy, balding grandpa with patience and discernment to spare, took his young grandson under his arm. The two set out to become anglers.

They joined the Grove City Sportsmen's Club a few miles from their home. Among the features of the outdoorsy social club was a two-acre private lake. The lake was surrounded by a gentle grass slope where all but a few middle-aged oak trees had been cleared. With the shoreline accessible and the lake stocked, shoreline sightings of Steve and Destin became frequent.

Fishing the same lake week after week, anglers get intimate with its features. At the same time, the lake's inhabitants get accustomed to the angler's lures. The drive to continue to catch fish prompted some creativity. Destin experimented with wading and later borrowed a canoe. Steve stood sentry on the shoreline, his green eyes peering through wire-rimmed glasses and recording every cast.

Not all of the watching happened at the lake. Fishing shows on weekend mornings were appointment viewing. During both shows, Grandpa sat on the loveseat, and Destin manned the couch, positioned straight opposite the 20-inch console TV. Iron City kid Destin could particularly relate to Mike Iaconelli, an emerging bass fishing pro at the time and a Philly fisherman with a Jersey attitude. If Iaconelli was hopping green pumpkin power worms, this kid from Grove City would try the same. Early Saturday morning was television's prime time at the Slencak house.

For nearly eight years, Destin and Grandpa Slencak were inseparable. When Steve's health began to fail, Destin even accompanied him

Steve Slenak and young Destin DeMarion.
Photo by Michele DeMarion.

to dialysis sessions. If fishing shows were not available, they reviewed fishing magazines together. Destin DeMarion's fishing buddy passed away in 2000 at the age of 66. DeMarion calls his years fishing with his grandfather "the good times."

Following Steve's passing, Destin started to crash neighboring farm ponds. He taught himself how to fish Rapalas, a brand name that serves as the local term for crankbaits. Through his high school years, he expanded his fishing repertoire. Destin's college major had another name, environmental science, but it was really fishing. He applied his degree on a bass fishing team. The results were promising enough to make fishing a career possibility.

POWER FISHING

Although DeMarion had a sentimental attachment to fishing, early success was hit-and-miss. He varied lures, presentations, riggings, equipment, and platforms. Bass were not always feeding, but he wanted to catch them anyway. He realized that he could potentially take advantage of the fish's innate response mechanism to achieve a more consistent bite.

Bass are cold-blooded creatures, and water temperature factors into their appetite. In 50-degree water, a bass may not feed more than once per week for metabolic purposes. As lakes and rivers warm into the mid-60s, energy usage increases. A 2002 study indicated that smallmouth bass can consume food equivalent to about 6 percent of their body weight each 60-degree day.[2] That would be like a human being consuming two bags of flour every day for two months. Bass feeding increases again when water temperatures hit the low 70s. Smallmouth bass daily consumption peaks near 8 percent of their body weight when water temperatures stay in this temperate zone. More extreme heat curtails the appetite. In places where water temperatures rise above 80 degrees, food consumption falls by half. Bass will hunt for forage amounting to 4 percent of their body weight. Lower oxygen solubility reduces energy needs.

---

2   Gregory W. Whitledge, Robert S. Hayward, and Charles F. Rabeni. "Effects of Temperature on Specific Daily Metabolic Demand and Growth Scope of SubAdult and Adult Smallmouth Bass." *Journal of Freshwater Ecology* 17:3, 353–361. 2002.

For a bass, hunger does not necessarily drive feeding. Bass are both predatory and territorial. They will attack targets of opportunity, and they will defend both their nests and their more often occupied safe spaces near laydowns and rocks. Power fishing enthusiasts try to invade a bass's environment with a lure that will make noise and disturb water. Anglers are trying for a reaction strike. They are not trying to entice a fish to eat. They make little attempt to match the natural size and speed of the forage.

Kevin VanDam was winning angler of the year awards in the early 2000s with this innovative method of power fishing. VanDam would visit 10 fishing sites in three hours, moving quickly from site to site. Contrary to the consensus at the time, he paid little attention to lure appearance. He focused on action. Even more trailblazing, he would seldom fish a lure all the way back to the boat. Once the lure exited the strike zone, he would reel it in. VanDam utilized action and speed to such success that ultimately he ended up in the bass fishing Hall of Fame. Destin watched VanDam on television and read about him in magazines.

Many anglers interpret VanDam's technique as "running and gunning." Having grown up bank fishing with the attention span typical of a young child, the idea of "running and gunning" greatly appealed to Destin. He is not the only one. Continual motion appeals to many bass anglers. Boats circling a lake while maintaining idle speed are frequent sights. They are probably attempting to power fish. Acre foot upon acre foot passes under their hulls. However, draining a trolling motor battery and turning the crank on a reel until it glows orange from friction misses the point of the exercise. The point is to catch fish, and to do so efficiently.

While some anglers embraced the movement aspect of power fishing, others tested the assumption that lure selection mattered little. Bryan Thrift achieved power fishing prominence by focusing on a singular bait. Thrift's choice was a chatterbait. With a curved metal blade positioned forward from a jig, a chatterbait makes noise and swims irregularly when it is quickly retrieved. The chatterbait proved revolutionary

Chatterbait. *Photo by Joe Kinnison.*

in agitating aggressive bass. Before internet stalking was a thing, Destin stalked Thrift, finding references to him in print and on video.

Power fishing describes itself in aggressive terms. Once these lures contact the surface, anglers retrieve them with velocity. This technique is called "burning" a bait. A steady retrieve is not the only way to move a bait quickly. As an alternative to burning, some anglers yank the lure, moving it extremely quickly for a short distance. Then, they gather line and repeat the process. This method is called "ripping." Whether burning or ripping, the power-fished lure is retrieved quickly. Cast. Burn. Cast. Rip. Cast.

Destin DeMarion's tempo is consistent and fast. He power fishes by motoring to a high-percentage site and firing three to five casts at a specific target. The target may be a rock, stump, or hump. After launching those casts, which may employ different lures from different rods, he evaluates the results of his sample. Fish or no fish, he guns the outboard and moves to the next site.

Expanding upon VanDam's plan but not circling the lake, Destin will make as many as 50 stops at preselected targets. Quick stops at multiple targets serve two purposes. First, he beats his competition to the best sites, and second, he learns how to be efficient with his fishing time that day. He tries to establish a pattern.

Power fishing can be accomplished with most fishing tackle. However, casting hard and aiming with precision works better with optimized gear. The best power-fishing rods are heavy-power, slow-action configurations. Braided line as heavy as 65-pound test is a typical power-fishing rigging. Lures should have action, flash, or sound. Having sampled nearly every power-fishing lure that appeared on TV or in a magazine, Destin DeMarion had an atypical choice in mind.

FROGS

While most power anglers burn chatterbaits and rip crankbaits, Destin DeMarion had a different attack. He adapted a finesse bait to a power-fishing technique. He throws a frog.

Most frogs are hollow plastic baits concealing two upturned hooks. The lure ties to the line between the eyes, near the nose. The outer shell comes in several shades of green, yellow, and brown attempting to mimic one of the 109 species of frogs found in North America. Most frog lures are buoyant; they float. Artificial frogs generally have streamers dangling from the point at which hind legs would be attached on the real amphibian. These streamers are often sparkly, like New Year's party favors.

Typical presentation of a frog is to cast the lure into an opening in vegetation. Anglers aim artificial frogs at pockets of water between lily pads and sparse grasses. Success is most often found by allowing the

Frog Psycho Toad. *By Strike King. Used with permission.*

lure to linger where it lands. Frequent frog anglers suggest waiting as long as 15 seconds before moving the lure. If the quarter-minute break does not draw a bite, the lure is retrieved slowly in a series of pulls and pauses. The action allows the streamers to extend and flutter before settling back into the water. Bass that do not rise to meet the lure in the open hole often tap the lure when it reaches the lakeside edge of the vegetation.

Anglers partial to frogs enjoy how bass attack the bait. The lure is a topwater presentation other than the streamers. Strikes on this lure can be particularly spectacular. Some bass attempt to stun frogs before sucking them into their mouths. To do so, the bass will rise with speed and headbutt the lure. The contact can be so violent that the frog is propelled several feet into the air. When it falls to the water, the momentarily disabled frog is consumed by the fish on its second pass. The power required to stun and consume the frog makes it a big fish lure.

Destin cautions that a trick in fishing with frog lures is knowing when to set the hook. When the strike is observed visually, anglers must do everything in their power to stop themselves from pulling back on the line. He controls the urge by reeling a half turn. When the bass makes its second pass and he perceives tension on the line, Destin knows he can then secure the fish.

Distinct from the classic frog presentation, Destin DeMarion usually fishes his frogs fast. Several frogs are tied to the tips of poles on either side of the deck of his boat. The rods are meticulously ordered according to his plan for use, and they are secured in place. One of his first casts delivers a buzzer toad. This lure comes in two forms. One is a soft plastic toad and the other could more properly be called a buzz bait with a plastic toad trailer. The buzzer toad is a movement lure that irritates fish with a high-pitched gurgling as the retrieve draws it over the top of the water. The blades give this bait similarity to the chatterbait, However, it has a different configuration. With a chatterbait, both the blade and the jig are on the same axis; whereas, the buzzer-toad positions the blade on a separate wire forward of the toad and about an inch higher.

The buzzer toad retrieve starts as soon as the lure splashes down. It does not dwell in the open hole in the vegetation. Loud and splashy, it tries to draw out a concealed bass. The first provocation does not always trigger even the most aggressive bass. Several casts to the same spot are often necessary. Subsequent casts vary the speed, normally from faster to slower.

Third and fourth casts to the same high-probability area may be made with other frogs. A hollow belly is often Destin's next lure to hit the water. This lure is a traditional artificial frog with painted details to make its appearance more lifelike. He twitches this frog by moving the rod tip, and he tries to change the direction of the lure with every twitch. If a few casts do not activate the fish, Destin moves to the next area.

Some anglers fish frogs selectively. Specific cover, such as lily pads, is uniquely targeted. Destin disagrees with this approach. He will throw a frog at docks, sections of riprap, shallow flats, and any promising shady spot. While throwing the rig anywhere, he will also cast it at nearly any season. Natural frogs are most active during early spring months when they spawn. While he takes advantage of those times, Destin has success fishing frogs early summer and fall. Destin DeMarion has modified the frog from being a seasonal finesse lure to being a multidimensional power lure.

VEGETATION

Destin's frogs target the surface of vegetation. He skims them above submerged weeds, and he pulls them through gaps and alleys in the thicket. Some bass hiding in cover will attack targets on the surface. While Destin's application of power methods is unique, artificial frogs are common lures for exploring the top layer of aquatic plant growths.

Many vegetation-focused anglers will employ a two-pronged strategy. They fish the top and bottom of a matte. When weeds grow to the surface, holes and gaps hold bass. However, greenery does not always protrude from the waves. Growth may stop a foot or more below the waterline. In these cases, vegetation can be fished by skimming lures

Destin Demarion fishing vegetation. *Courtesy of B.A.S.S.*
Used with permission.

over the top of the salad. Lipless crankbaits are popular lures for this
approach.

Fishing the bottom of a weed bed requires an entirely different set
of equipment than fishing the top. The bottom has a tangle of stalks. A
heavy weight is required to penetrate the top cover and sink through the
stems. Sinkers as large as 1½ ounces can do the job. These weights punch
through the surface foliage and draw the lure down through the thicket.
High-test fishing line is needed to pull them out.

Although heavier weights are generally required to target bass at the
base of weeds, grasses, and lily pads, the lures themselves may be smaller
than the ones used to attract surface strikes. The reason for the small
lures is small forage. Tiny creatures mass below the greenery. A typical
presentation would be a 3½-inch artificial crawfish. Texas-rigging to
the heavy weight keeps the lure as close as possible to the base of the
plants.

Fishing on the bottom amid vegetation is prone to snagging.
Weedless lures lessen the likelihood of hang-ups, but twisted stems seem
to have a tendency to envelope baits. Good prospective fishing holes can
be ruined by dragging caught weeds or by boat trips into the greenery
for lure extraction. To minimize snags, fishing the bottom of vegetation is best accomplished in open holes and at the lakeside edge of the
growth.

Weed beds can grow quite large. When vegetation extends for a hundred yards or more, it can be difficult to determine where in the mass of plants to find fish. Holes and gaps may be plentiful. Alternatively, they may not exist at all. In situations such as these, skilled anglers improve their odds by searching for oddities.

Oddities may include variations and mixtures. Variations may be protrusions or recessions. Some sections of the weeds will finish closer to shore or farther from shore. These differences in the shape of the vegetation can create mini-pockets and greenery points. Pockets and points hold fish.

Weed mixtures offer another type of variety. Combinations of different types of weeds hold fish. Look for areas where grasses intersect lily pads, for example. The combination of textures offers unique habitat. If a mixture of weeds is not present, bass will gravitate toward areas with a greater-than-average combination of dead and live plants. More camouflage is typical of these areas, with a mix of greens, yellows, and browns. While color options multiply amid live and decaying plants, hiding places also broaden. Live plants reach upward to light, while dead ones topple and sink. This creates protective cover at two different depths. Mixtures of dead and live vegetation will have varied habitat, which often attracts more fish.

If forage, shade, and oxygen generation can be found, the bass will be present. Thickets of vegetation offer all three. When Destin is power fishing from site to site, he selects open holes, edges, and oddities among the vegetation for his stops.

LAKE CHICKAMAUGA

Not only has Destin DeMarion adapted his own version of power fishing, he has also optimized his equipment to the task. Destin drives a 21-foot Phoenix bass boat. Before every fishing trip, he focuses on reducing weight. A lighter boat is a faster boat, so he has only the tackle necessary for the day. He fills only enough gas to get to the right fishing areas and return. Destin seldom leaves the dock with fuel tanks full. A few extra horsepower helps him to run and gun. He moves fast on his favorite lake, Lake Chickamauga.

"The Chick" is consistently rated as one of the Top 10 bass lakes in the United States. It has been steadily climbing that list. Bassmaster rated the lake the second-best fishery in the country in 2020. The increased attention has generated significant fishing pressure. Weekends can be crowded with anglers, making the bass finicky.

The Tennessee River impoundment makes a blue S-curve through the southern Smoky Mountains. The lake is rimmed by leafy hills. (Fall foliage can be stunning). The rolling terrain extends underwater. The mounded habitat is covered with enough vegetation to satisfy at least one angler of artificial frogs.

Lake Chickamauga. *By Destin DeMarion.*

The Tennessee Valley Authority (TVA) built Lake Chickamauga in 1940, and its primary purpose is to provide power to the region. Fulfilling its purpose, the TVA regularly runs water both into and out of the lake to turn the turbines for the generating stations. This water movement creates a current in the lake, and the bass are often activated by the moving water.

The bass can get quite large. Florida strain bass, the largest of the North American bass species, are stocked in the lake. Although the Florida strain bass are not native, they mix with the homegrown bass, giving the lake good genetics. The largemouth bass record for the lake is 15 pounds, three ounces, caught in 2015. Another whopper, weighing 14.5 pounds, was caught in 2017. It takes a five-fish stringer weighing nearly 30 pounds to be competitive in many spring tournaments on Lake Chickamauga,

Tournaments are not limited to the spring. They are nonstop. The most common starting/weigh-in point is the Dayton Boat Dock on the north end of the lake about 38 miles from Chattanooga, Tennessee. The Dayton Boat Dock access is a practical but not a beautiful spot. A long riprap peninsula is its main feature. The bay holds a hundred tournament-ready bass boats, and a slough connects to the lake. One of our recommended guides, Scott Patton, frequently launches from Dayton.

Although the boat launch has an industrial feel, Dayton has better features. Visitors might explore the preserved Rhea County Courthouse where the Scopes case was decided. William Jennings Bryan and Clarence Darrow argued the famous lawsuit in that court room. Following the Scopes ruling, evolution was first taught in US schools.

Dayton is an active town. It is a byway on several motorcycle tours. The Trail of Tears, Fall Creek Falls, Tale of the Dragon, and Cherohala Skyway are all reachable treks starting from Dayton. The rumble of Harleys is a regular presence in the city. If the open road calls to you, motorcycle rentals are available.

The Blue Water Resort is the premier lodging choice in the area. The resort has a lodge, log cabins, and camp sites all arrayed on a grassy point. The resort is angler friendly, and water access betters that of the Dayton Boat Dock. Tackle and live bait are available on-site.

While most anglers start at Dayton, Destin prefers to fish mid-lake. About 20 miles south of Dayton (20 miles north of Chattanooga) sits the town of Soddy Daisy, Tennessee. Soddy Daisy the nearest town to the Chester Frost Park. The boat ramp there is a nice access for traveling anglers.

The ramp itself extends from a lush island on the west side of the lake. The manicured lakefront has a pier and a playground. The park area is quiet and nice. Destin occasionally stays in one of the 200 lakefront campsites.

It requires a short drive to find food in the area. The trip to Steve's Landing is worth it. The restaurant sits lakeside near a marina, and boat parking is available for those who prefer to travel via watercraft. The plantation-style building has a wood-fenced deck. On the elevated surface, green metal patio furniture offers some outdoor seating. Ribs are the specialty of the house, and Steve's is one of those places where having dessert is a must.

Once launching your boat at Chester Frost, Dallas Bay is an easy run to the northwest. It has extensive largemouth bass fishing terrain. The north shore of the bay has extensive shallows. These six- to 12-foot-deep flats areas are accentuated by a line of boat lifts. The lifts extend several yards away from shore and most are covered with roofs. The bass have space to roam and places to hide.

Dark-bottomed, green-tinged Dallas Bay has marsh areas on its west side. Forage can change near these wetlands. Careful navigation is required, as depths range from 1 to 3 feet.

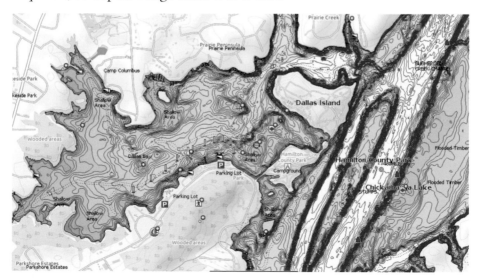

Dallas Bay. Lake Chickamauga. *Copyright 2021 Garmin Ltd or its subsidiaries. All rights reserved. Used with permission.*

The south side of this large bay is largely undeveloped. Trees line the shores. Three small landmasses jut above the water, providing some depth variation. The offshore rock formation has a reef-like layout. Bass tuck behind the rock ledges. Getting them out can be tough on your fishing line.

Bass seem to like the shallow terrain of Dallas Bay in the morning hours. Since the bay has little depth, it warms quickly. As the morning ages to afternoon, the fish disappear under boat lifts and rock formations, or they flee to the channel.

Later in the day, Chickamauga bass are known to stack up on ledges in the river channel. Once out of Dallas Bay, a short run down lake gets anglers to Wolftever Creek. The 22-foot-deep section of the lake can be an attractive spot. In that area, creeks intersect the nearby riverbed. Although the underwater terrain is promising, this bend in the lake can be difficult to fish. Boat traffic is extensive, and the wakes can be disruptive.

Guide services will present more options to visiting anglers. It is not unusual to hire a guide for a day, and fish solo for a second day. In recent years, guides have been booked solid for May and June. It takes some advance planning to secure a date. The best guide services help visiting anglers handle the fishing pressure by supplying light tackle and finding out-of-the-way locations. The fishing guides listed below are recommended.

Select Chickamauga Fishing Guide Services

Chattanooga Fishing Guides	423-240-5389	kkite23@epbfi.com
Scenic City Fishing Charters	423-509-4655	richard@sceniccityfishing.com
Scott Patton Fishing	731-227-9499	scottpattonfishing@yahoo.com
Welch Guide Service	705-455-2323	info@welchsguideservice.com

ADAPTATION

Back in the days when *American Idol* was a hit television show, one of the highest compliments paid to an emerging artist was that they were able to adapt a standard song and "make it their own." The contestants would make small changes to lyrics, rhythms, or notes. The alterations recast the song to favor the artist's individual style.

Performing an adaptation of a previous hit is called "covering" a song. Covering songs is common, at times caricature. The *Glee* television series and the *Pitch Perfect* feature films are based on the practice. The best cover songs elevate the source material.

Destin DeMarion studied the source material from the great anglers in the history of power fishing. Then he made it his own. He adapted techniques to fit the lures he likes and the vegetation he prefers to fish. Destin customized traditional lure retrievals to give them an element of uniqueness.

Each angler has a distinctive combination of personal traits and life experiences. Taking those inputs and creating something new is a feature of the human species. Other than opposable thumbs, crafting of our own awareness separates us from the rest of the animal kingdom. Programmed for high-level thought, humans possessing originality is generally not distinctive. Channeling it to a productive outcome is the trick. Casting a thumb drive hooked to the end of a leader may be creative, but it is not likely to catch fish.

The cover song example was purposeful. The adaptation would be impossible without a thorough understanding of the original material. In this way, originality has a legacy element. In fact, it is impossible to recognize an idea as a truly new innovation unless one knows what came before. New patents, for example, require a search of prior art. Amateur anglers are advised to do their homework so they recognize when their innate creativity reveals something original.

Along with appreciation for the prior art of fishing, angling originality requires self-awareness. Detail the aspects of fishing at which you excel. For example, search baits or, alternatively, finesse presentations may inspire you. A person in command of their strengths can better innovate in those areas.

Aligning fishing legacy with self-awareness happens best during unstructured time on the water. An active tournament schedule can work against originality. Time pressure seldom fosters expansive thought. Get on the water and give your mind a chance to work.

LEGACY

Guided by his grandfather throughout his childhood, Destin is trying to pay it forward as an adult. When he is not fishing in tournaments, he can be found providing fishing instruction. Destin is a natural explainer who delivers information with a nonthreatening shoulder shrug. If he needs to be insistent, he raises his shoulders and adds open hand gestures to punctuate his remarks. His voice inflections are pastoral. If not a fishing instructor, he might be a favorite teacher at a grade school.

Destin provides his gentle guidance working on the St. John's River near Jacksonville, Florida. He works for a friend's guide service navigating the cypress-draped, slow-moving intercoastal waterway hunting bass from January through May. During the rest of the season, he drives 75 miles north from home to take clients on Lake Erie fishing excursions.

Learning how to provide instruction has proven to be a challenge equal to learning to fish. At first, Destin wanted his customers to catch

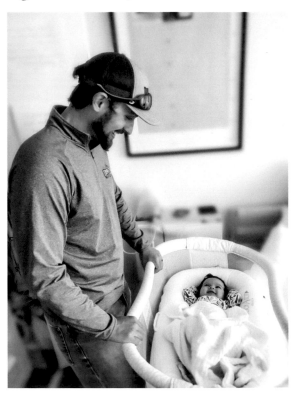

Destin DeMarion and child. *Photo by Meghan DeMarion.*

fish the way he did. Given different levels of experience among the anglers, "do what I do" did not prove to be a success path. He has since learned to urge his clients toward success while letting them figure out the techniques that work for them individually. His grandfather must be smiling.

Off the water, Destin has started recording tutorials as a new way to share his passion. He plans to add two or three videos per month as a resource to help people start bass fishing. His latest submission explains when to use various types of crankbait bills. At his production rate, he should have his teaching method refined by the time his newborn daughter is ready to start wetting a line. In case you were wondering, fishing videos can be effective tools to soothe infants to sleep.

CHAPTER 14
Acquisition:
Something acquired or gained.[1]

Finding fish can be the greatest challenge in the sport. Even the most experienced anglers have days where they struggle to pinpoint the location of bass. The quarry will change terrain, change depths, and change directions on small variations in environmental conditions. Fish found yesterday may not be in the same place today. Water temperature is usually a good guide to bass haunts, but weather extremes such as wind, rain, and full sun alter the pattern.

Since fish reposition as conditions change, it is recommended that anglers begin each new fishing day with a search. The general rule of thumb is to look for signs of life. Signs of life can come from birds circling, ripples on the surface, or rushes against the shore. A few casts of a search bait will confirm the pattern you expect or at least verify the presence of bass in a chosen area.

WATER TEMPERATURE

Bass move seasonally, and water temperature can provide a bearing as to where to locate the migrating fish. If the water temperature is in the 50s, bass will be on the flats. At these shoulder season temperatures, bass move shallow to feed and spawn. If the water temperature is in the 60s, bass will position near structure. This temperature range gets comfortable for the cold-blooded creatures, and the bass choose ambush locations from

---

1   Retrieved November 7, 2020, from https://www.merriam-webster.com/dictionary
    /acquisition

which to feed. If the water temperature is in the 70s, bass will migrate to underwater slopes. Steep underwater terrain enables bass to ascend to feed and descend to hide without expending much energy. The edges of river and lake points often offer some of the slopes. If the water temperature is in the 80s, bass will congregate at the thermocline. The fish will stay deep to find the best combination of oxygen and temperature.

Absolute temperatures are not the only driver of fish location. Differences in temperature, as slight as one or two degrees, can cause repositioning among the fish. For example, a shallow cove may warm more quickly than the main body of a lake. That few extra degrees of temperature can be significant enough for the bass to travel to that area. Degree differences also work in the opposite direction. That few degrees of additional temperature will repel bass in hot weather. The fish will flee 81-degree water for 78-degree water.

For anglers who would prefer not to parse degree gradients and for those without the aid of electronics, there is a simple way to locate the fish. Think of the optimal temperature for the bass being 65 degrees. Identify parts of the water body closest to that figure and concentrate your fishing efforts in those areas. Shading, water movement, springs, and relative depth may all factor in to producing something close to the optimal temperature range.

WIND

Windy conditions often activate bass. To the extent that the wind causes wave action on the surface of the water, absorbed oxygen levels in the water rise. With more oxygen content in their environment, bass have more energy.

Not only are the fish more active, they tend to rise higher in the water column, sometimes very near the surface. The choppy surface often produced by wind keeps the fish from being spotted from above. With birds thwarted, bass can rise and roam the shallows.

With more of the body of water available to the high-on-oxygen bass, they expand their normal range and increase their food consumption. Gusty conditions can fill the shallows with prey. Baitfish are often unable to counter the strong push of water against a windward shoreline. A current driven by the wind-propelled waves can herd small fish into shallow area. A large population of baitfish somewhat captive to conditions can draw predators.

While bass will likely be feeding on downwind shorelines, presenting baits can be a challenge for anglers. Bass generally maneuver themselves to face upwind. With this posture, whatever food the weather drives to the shore, the bass will be in position to slurp it up. The challenge for the angler is that the natural location for a boat is upwind, farther offshore than the fish. Casting lures to the shore and retrieving them forward past the tails of the fish may trigger a few reaction strikes, but the direction that the lure would be moving is unnatural. The better presentation would be to allow baits to drift shallow driven by the wind and waves. Anglers might employ bobbers to accomplish this drift, or they could utilize weightless, soft plastic lures. Drifting may require atypical gear, and being slow, it may be difficult to maintain boat position. As an alternative, anglers can launch lures parallel to the shoreline, allowing for some downwind drift as they work lures across the shoreline flat. Casting across the wind can get very frustrating as the air pressure bends the line. For those up for the challenge, it can produce bites with a more typical cast and retrieve.

RAIN

Clouds building on the horizon often mean good things for anglers in the short term. Bass are sensitive to barometric pressure, which drops prior to a rainstorm. The phenomenon is caused by a high-pressure air front building above a mass of low pressure. As the high pressure moves in, the barometer readings fall.

Growing cloud cover provides an opportunity for fish to move toward the surface, and the falling pressure exerts less strain on their swim bladders. Less energy is required to feed, and bass will rise from the depths to attack topwater targets. Inclined to rise against lower resistance, the fish get another break when the raindrops fall. Drops break the surface tension of the water, again shielding bass from surface predators.

While retrieving baits slightly below the surface of the water will likely catch bass early in a rainstorm, something with a little bit of flash will stand out against the dark skies and dimpled surface. Swim baits suit this purpose.

The pattern changes as the storm persists. After several minutes of steady rain, water will start to fill gullies, creeks, and storm sewers. This water flows into the larger rivers and lakes. The new water makes several changes to the lake environment. First, the new water is often colder than the static pool in the body of water. Especially in the summer, a rush of cold water is a welcome happening for the fish. The cold water often gushes with worms and bugs, providing a new set of targets for the bass. Finally, the flowing tributaries are often muddy. The muddy inflow does not disperse immediately. Distinct zones separating muddy effluent from clear water set up. Transition areas where dark water meets light liquid can create new ambush settings for the bass.

When fishing during a rain, watch tributaries for the inflows to begin. Once a steady flow starts, anglers should position offshore from the inflow. Altering lure selections from those utilized before the rain, anglers would change to try to mimic the forage coming from the gush. As the water starts to muddy, back away from the shoreline and try to maintain casting distance away from any color change in the water.

Extensive rainfall changes the pattern again. Rising water levels can open new terrain. To the extent that shoreline grasses and bushes are flooded, bass may move extremely shallow to explore the new environments.

The downside of rain events is that once the rain stops and the inflows slow, fish often turn inactive. That inactivity can last as long as three days. The positive conditions that moved the fish into feeding positions all reverse. The barometric pressure rises after the storm clears. The waters mix and levelize, and the gush of new forage stops.

FULL SUN

Anglers can dread bright, sunny summer days. Under such conditions, fish will emerge at dawn and dusk, and not often in between. Next-level anglers can catch them during the in-betweens.

Bass feed in the shade. The phrase is an easy one to remember, and it is a good guide to finding fish on a sunny day. As the sun moves through the sky, shoreline features create shadows. Overhanging trees darken the water, and cliffsides cut off the sun angle. The bass will locate in these dappled areas.

Anglers who hug the eastern shore are likely to extend the early-morning bite. The rising sun will illuminate the western shore first. Once the sun rises, anglers are advised to shift focus and concentrate on sun protection provided by tree cover. Some pockets get sun last due to either orientation, geography, or shadows from surrounding foliage or buildings. Dwelling in these areas as the sun continues its ascent can elongate a bite. Taking a similar approach, anglers should target the emerging shadows on the western shoreline in the afternoon.

Shade and shadows can buy anglers a few extra minutes at the tails of the day. However, those minutes may not be sufficient to fill live wells. Thankfully, underwater structure can also provide shade. Crappie, part of the bass forage base, is famous for occupying the shady side of brush piles. For anglers operating side-image sonar with the sun at their backs, the sonar shadows provide a good approximation of what the fish might experience in terms of sun protection. Where the baitfish go, the bass follow. Look on the shady side of submerged cover. Bass relating to cover will not stray far from its protection on sunny days. It is incumbent upon anglers to present lures as close as possible to the shady side of the brush pile. Once the lure is delivered, "soaking" the lure by letting it sit in place for a full minute or more can improve bite rates.

When the sun is high in the sky, it is important to remember that the summertime bass that are not relating tightly to cover will bunch into large schools. These schools rove rivers and lakes, and they occasionally appear near the surface. When they do, anglers will see the water boil and churn. The churn will move relatively quickly, often in unpredictable directions. The churn will also disappear for a time. It will reemerge often enough that a boat with a diligent captain can follow its path. Casting into the churn can pick off a few members of the school on days with full sun. Next-level anglers keep a rig on deck to be ready for such opportunities. A dark lure that looks like a baitfish is a good choice.

MATCH THE HATCH

Most of the weather-driven changes in bass location are really changes in the position of their food source. Wind pins food to the shoreline. Rain brings new forage into the river or lake. Sun drives baitfish into the shadows. In a similar way, bug hatches are natural-moving feasts.

Bug hatches occur throughout the temperate months, but some of the more prominent ones occur in the summer. Mayflies and dobsonflies are among several species that hatch by rising from the bottom of a body of water. Subspecies of mayflies, called drakes, emerge in various colors within several weeks during the summer. Brown, Yellow, Golden, and Green are the varied shades. During a typical hatch, thousands of flies emerge in the last hours of a day. The flies rise from the bottom and dawdle momentarily on the surface while their wings dry. These occasions provide surface targets for bass feeding frenzies.

When they emerge, cicadas inhabit overhanging trees. After two months, they begin to expire, and the bugs fall into the water. When the big bugs pelt the water, bass gorge on them.

Bug hatches seldom occur all in one place. For example, mayflies may emerge in one cove but appear nowhere else. They hatch in another area of the lake or river two weeks later. Bass tend not to move long distances, but they will migrate a little for a bug hatch. Anglers who can identify signs of an upcoming hatch can certainly locate fish. Nature journals and farmer's almanacs do a pretty good job of targeting dates for bug hatches. Orvis makes a handy reference chart. Finding the right area of your lake may be the trick. However, once you have found them, bug hatches can occur over periods of up to three days.

Merely locating a bug hatch may not be sufficient for you to catch your limit. The fish can be dialed in to the appearance of the rising nymph (they see a lot of them) as well as the particular shape of the duns on the surface. Casting a lure that does not look like either a nymph or a duns is a waste of time. Tube baits can make a fair imitation of the larva, with a center mass and some tendrils. Jointed crankbaits can be confused for the emergent flies. Plausible shape will get the angler bites. More than most fishing occasions, color remains a key consideration during a hatch. Mayflies might be bright yellow on the north side of a lake and yellow-brown on the south side. Anglers who can match the hatch can land the fish.

BIG FISH

The biggest bass behave differently than smaller fish. Targeting the lunkers necessitates adaptions to strategy. Anglers aiming for the biggest bass reset their approach. Big-game hunters fish deeper, move slower, and sling bigger baits.

Big bass dwell in deeper water than the smaller editions of the species. While five to 10 feet is a productive depth to fish most bass, the biggest fish spend most of their time about five feet deeper. In the deep, they can suspend away from the more frequent activity on the flats and in the shallows. Baits that swim deeper and fall faster are necessary in the quest for the bigger animals.

Suspending is what big bass do. The lack of effort is a hallmark of the lunker class. The fish are sedentary. In most seasons, they only move one or two times per day. They emerge only to feed. Outside of those brief movement periods, the big ones hug cover and stay relatively still.

To support these long periods of inactivity, big bass often have a lair. The fish gravitate to the most complex and extensive cover in a waterway. Big bass will tuck in tight to brush, and they will seldom feed when hunkered down.

When big largemouths emerge to hunt, they go big. Their lairs are near transportation routes, creek beds, and points. They watch passing schools, and they emerge to attack the largest baitfish. The slovenly fish attempt to maximize the hunting effort by pursuing the largest protein source that they can find. The old saying that to catch big bass you need a big bait is well founded. Big bass are looking for one big bite.

Although sizable lures might attract big fish, size is not everything in big bass fishing. The fish have a preference for large quarry, but the fish are also unusually wary of anything unnatural in their environment. Big baits fished inelegantly will likely not work. In addition, big baits that do not resemble forage are counterproductive. These fish have survived by being cagey, and they will return to their hiding spots at the slightest provocation.

Finding the biggest bass requires patient study. Anglers must locate complex cover in mid-depths near transportation routes. These areas are usually farther offshore than traditional bass fishing venues. An angler has to train herself to find typical bass habitat, and then back off to deeper water. Once finding the right locale, the angler tries to discern the one or two times of day that the bass feeds. Big fish may not share the dusk-and-dawn rhythm of their smaller counterparts. When big ones do emerge, large baits need to be presented naturally and slowly.

Water temperature, weather patterns, and forage emergence dictate where to find fish. These factors lead anglers to most bass, but the biggest bass play by their own rules. Next-level anglers are flexible, versatile, and creative in applying their methods to catching lunkers.

Epilogue

Personal qualities separate next-level bass anglers from amateurs. The most accomplished anglers have a structured approach; they are keen to fish physiology; they are versatile; they are focused; their originality has a forum.

Each personal quality has physical aspects, though most people have adequate physical tools for angling. Sense acuity may be the single most essential physical element. Techniques for organizing and optimizing sense stimuli appear throughout this book.

Physical tools aside, building advanced angling capability is mostly accomplished through mental exercises and relationship leverage. Journaling, recitation, experimentation, and improvisation are all types of brain training. Mentorship and legacy are types of relationship training. Once utilized, all of these tools elevate angling capability.

To poke fun at myself, I would say that a critic of these innovative techniques might be reminded of a classic musical. In *The Music Man*, the character Professor Harold Hill sells musical instruments.[1] Actually playing the instruments is foreign to the salesman. He invents a "think system" in which children visualize how to play trumpets and trombones. The think system works only in the sense that it makes noise and mollifies expectant parents.

Let me assure you that next-level bass fishing is not a think system. The training is mental and relational. However, to be effective, it must

---

1 Willson, M. "The Music Man." Performance by Broderick, M. The Music Man (TV Movie 2003)—IMDb

be employed in actual practice. Time on the water selecting strategies and delivering lures has no substitute. To draw on the analogy, readers have learned the notes and the scales. Now, it is time to practice.

I pointed out earlier that fishing may be the only sport in which practice is looked down upon. Next-level anglers practice. They practice on and off the water. Look online for a video of Pam Martin-Wells flipping a jig into a saucepan if you need proof. Brandon Palaniuk believes that the more he practices, the more instinctual he becomes. That really is the point of next-level bass fishing, to internalize enhancements in knowledge, approach, and purpose to the point that they become instinctual.

START SMALL

When it comes to integrating any one of these new skills, I recommend starting small. If an opportunity is available to you, I recommend that your first practice sessions take place at a location where catching fish is easy. Early in my bass fishing education, I was given regular access to a friend's farm ponds. This collection of two- to 10-acre lakes was stocked and seldom-used. Hungry and naïve bass will bite most anything, and constant action affords an angler multiple chances to sample new learnings while facing few consequences. The forgiving environment helped me figure out how lures worked and what retrieves prompted strikes.

A lake full of rabid bass might be just the place to experiment with a seldom used cadence. It may also be the right spot to concentrate on environmental signals. What are the bugs doing? Are they rising from the bottom or descending from the trees? Are they moving or staying still? What color are they? Are they only in certain places on the lake? Try it.

You might try casting something completely original, like a Merthiolate twisty-tail worm hooked wacky-style. Varying bait configurations is one way to experiment. Changing between fishing styles is another. If finesse angling is your usual approach, try power fishing. Moving unusually quickly between prospective sites would also be good training. In my experience, active fish provide the best environments for building confidence in the progress you have made developing your personal qualities.

Once you have mastered a stocked pond, move up to a larger body of water. Today, my home lake is a 150-acre impoundment in eastern Missouri. It is a midsize lake by my own definition. For a lake this size, a plan is necessary. You might focus on a particular type of terrain or a certain structure. A lake of this size has several biomes. Rely on your senses to identify the different forage in various creeks and coves. This is a good environment for structuring a fishing day and tracking your progress.

After successfully analyzing a midsize lake, give the big ones a try. The lakes visited by professional anglers are vast and intimidating. Boating skills are as important as fishing skills. I cannot imagine solo navigating the vast waters of a Toledo Bend or a Lake Moultrie. It makes sense that such massive bodies of water hold more big fish. However, finding them presents a huge challenge for an almost next-level angler. If you are ready to try it, plan on lots of preparatory map work, and do not be afraid to enlist a guide. Making a vast body of water small by targeting the spots that both hold bass and fit your fishing style preference is key.

Lake size is not the only variable to consider when putting new techniques into practice. Different pools of water have different levels of clarity. Some have verdant plant life while some have none at all. Some are littered with stumps. Some have only their underwater slopes to provide habitat for fish. Not all methods fit every body of water. Design an approach appropriate to the habitat.

I'll use my home lake as an example. Lake Aspen has a soft bottom. The only trees and root balls are a few hundred structures recently installed by the fishing club. Holiday weekend boat traffic is substantial. The water is normally stained, and sometimes, it gets downright murky. An algae bloom starts in late summer. Otherwise, little plant life emerges from the bottom.

In putting into practice some of the technical suggestions from the pros, I find myself limited by the circumstances of my lake. A frog in a vegetation-free body of water is out of place. My lake does have creek channels, a take where material was removed to create the dam, and some underwater structure. A swim jig is ideal for this application. The advice from Pam Martin-Wells to use a shaky head when lakes get pressured has paid off for me on several occasions.

Those frequenting clear lakes might gravitate to the sight-fishing cycle. For clear-water anglers, swim baits may be second nature. In these same situations, power-fishing techniques may not be applicable. Depending on the nature of your water, some of the tips will work for you and some will not. Try what you can.

TRAIN NEXT-LEVEL QUALITIES

While not all of the gear selection and strategy advice has equal application, the practices advised to enhance personal qualities are of use for everyone. I make a regular effort to work on my personal fishing qualities.

In my experience, professional anglers are unusually sensate. To the extent novice anglers can better realize and interpret sensations, chances of next-level angling results drastically improve. In working on acuity myself, I have learned that my senses have varied levels of subtlety. For example, my sense of smell is poor. I would not even notice the COVID-19 symptom of the loss of smell.

Working around a bad sniffer is one of the easier adaptations in fishing. I know to be careful with scents on my hands. In addition, when I do detect a smell, like the fetor of a new garlic-impregnated plastic worm right out of the bag, I know the smell is a strong one for the fish.

Although smell is a lost cause for me, visual acuity is not. Having employed the eye workouts and eye-training exercises, I can tell you that they work. In fact, I am blown away by how well they work. Details that I have never seen prior to training are now evident.

My visual training comes from focusing on a maple tree, just off the edge of the patio in my backyard. As the exercises suggest, I try to view the tree on a leaf by leaf basis. It is particularly interesting in the spring when leaves unfold, and in the fall when the green shades to yellow. This tree has clusters of helicopter seeds seasonally. I concentrate on those samara duos to the point of seeing the black, wiry stems with a nub on each outside end. With this sort of examination, one gets sensitive to movement, almost annoyed by it. The wind can change the positions of the target stem. That reaction to motion helps me most when on the water.

Among the other personal qualities characteristic of next-level anglers, I find that I am in pretty good shape on structure. My personal fishing journal is in its ninth year. My discipline is to write a page at the end of every fishing outing. I sit and write for five minutes just after I stow my rods.

Writing at the end of a trip is only half of a structured approach. Although I seldom bring the journal on board my boat, I refer to it before setting out on most trips. After previewing upcoming weather data, I browse the journal for conditions that appear to be similar to those expected. I remind myself which lures worked, and I review which parts of the lake were productive. With that information, I know which lures I am starting with and which lake features I am targeting.

While strong in some areas of structure, I have shown weaknesses in other aspects. I discovered that I would stay in unproductive locations for far too long. According to my preset plan, I used to go to where I think the fish should be. On occasions when they are not present, I would continue to beat the bank with cast after cast. Now, the structured approach has me pause my casting at least every hour. I evaluate the number and quality of bites, and I force a stay-or-go decision. My fishing time is getting more efficient, perhaps even next-level.

While bettering my personal management of structure, the next-level quality of physiology continues to amaze me. I have unhooked bass so white-shaded that I wondered about their health. With some education on pigment, I realize that I am seeing camouflage in stained water. In addition, I am getting some clues on depth.

My problem with focus is that I do not think I possess a standout fishing skill. I cannot seem to stop myself from varying the lures I cast, even if one is consistently working. While inclined to variety at the expense of focus, I have benefited from being a mentee. I had lots of fishing help with worms and bobbers as a child. I have found anglers of all sorts to be forthcoming with good advice. I cannot remember an outing where I did not learn something from my fishing partner.

Perhaps this goes with my lack of focus, but I think frequently changing partners has provided me with some of the most valuable fishing insights. Another discipline, dancing, explains this point best. My wife and I took ballroom dancing classes a few years ago. The instructor required us to change partners every week. Her point was that each dancer moves a little differently. You learn by adjusting. The same point applies to fishing. The more often you have a partner, the better. "Dancing with Myself" is so 1980s passé.[2]

I do have a word of caution on guides. At times, I have sought advice by booking trips with local professional guides. I do appreciate my guide friends, but I have generally found these outings to be disappointing from a teaching perspective. Clients give bigger tips if they catch more fish. Guides have go-to lures and go-to fishing holes. Most seem to be at a loss if their first options stop working. More importantly from a mentor perspective, guides try to protect their secrets rather than coach their anglers. In my experience, guides are not mentors.

Those that achieve originality, guided by versatility and legacy, are the ultimate next-level anglers. It takes a lot of study and a lot of practice to get to that point. Those anglers are in position to advance themselves and further the sport. I'd like to think that I have created an innovative cadence. However, I may not yet be ready for my attempt at a national tour.

JOIN A BASS CLUB

Through offering many pairing opportunities, bass clubs are one of the best ways to enhance your versatility. Deepwater and shallow-water specialists might share a boat. Boaters often host non-boaters. A crankbait aficionado could find herself with a disciple of slow-moving soft plastics. Some of these parings may be trying, but they will add perspective on your way to becoming a next-level angler.

---

2   Idol, B., and James, T. "Dancing with Myself." Performed by Idol, B. Chrysalis. 1981.

Anglers interested in building next-level skills, but not ready to turn professional would find welcome in a bass club. Most US states have bass fishing clubs. Often, clubs are organized by cities or regions, but some are denominational, ethnic, age-level, or military membership groups. States with the largest bass angler populations count nearly 60 fishing groups.

My personal affiliation is with the Innsbrook Fishing Club. The Innsbrook Fishing Club is a large fishing organization. Its membership nears 200 anglers. The club has an annual habitat construction day, it manages fish populations, and it holds occasional tournaments. Although membership is sizable, typically about 40 anglers participate in the tournaments. When fishing, we mostly target bass. However, we have the occasional catfish tournament or green sunfish harvest.

That Innsbrook Fishing club tournament roster is still large relative to the size of the majority of bass clubs around the country. About 20 members would be an average size club. However, they need not be that big. On the small end, clubs can be established with as few as six anglers.

The majority of bass clubs are tournament-oriented. The Innsbrook Club hosts two events of our own and participates in two other resort area events. Most other clubs are more active. Monthly fishing events are more common, especially in states having warmer climates. On the high-frequency extreme, a club in Florida holds 24 tournaments each year.

For those clubs hosting events, single-day fishing competitions are the norm. Tournament durations vary, but six hours of fishing time is common. Fishing a single event is perfectly acceptable, but many clubs have season-long series. They accumulate results over several tournaments. Modeling themselves on the Bassmaster Classic event, high scorers are invited to a championship. For several clubs, the feature tournament is a two-day event.

Not only do anglers have opportunities to compete within their clubs, but some regions also offer intraclub fishing matches. Regions assemble their best club anglers into teams of, typically, six. Those groups fish in statewide contests.

Not all bass club tournaments are advancement-oriented. Some are for fun. These winners capture only bragging rights. For example, my club has no-fee tournaments, and it awards trophies.

At the other end of the spectrum, some club tournaments are cash-focused. For the cash motivated, prizes can reach five-figure sums. These tournaments normally have high entry fees, however. Clubs typically set tournament fees to either attract or repel those motivated by prize money. Whatever your competitive fire and financial resource, a bass club tournament option is likely available.

Even tournaments with cash entry fees are not moneymakers for the hosting clubs in most cases. It is typical for a club to boast of returning 100 percent of the entry fees in prizes to the winning anglers. Since tournaments are not a significant funding source, most bass clubs charge annual dues. Dues near $50 per member are customary. Fees cover costs such as administration, meeting space, and stewardship efforts. Most clubs hold regular meetings. Care for the animals and the water systems are frequent topics.

Part of any good club's mission is to grow the sport of fishing. To promote the sport that they love, most clubs hold outreach events. Kids instruction, equipment tune-ups, lake conservation projects, or stocking programs are not unusual. With efforts like these, clubs help maintain the lakes they frequent. Doing so, bass clubs are most often an asset to their lake and river communities.

Joining a club may be as simple as contacting club leadership. However, some clubs do not have open enrollment. Restrictive clubs may require proof of fishing ability so that their anglers are comfortably matched. Extending beyond restrictions, some clubs are exclusive. Exclusive clubs control their quality by limiting the absolute number of anglers permitted. For example, I have found a club that approves only 12 members at any one time. Occasionally, clubs have demographic or experiential requirements. A few clubs (mostly in Florida) restrict membership to those 55 and older. Separately, some bass clubs are for military and ex-military members only. While some clubs are restrictive or exclusive, most are open to anglers trying to advance next-level skills.

Some links to bass fishing clubs appear in Appendix II. Make contact and progress to your next level of bass fishing.

APPENDIX I:
References and Additional Reading

Chapter 1
Temperament

Bennett, Art, and Lariane Bennett. *The Temperament God Gave You*. Sophia Institute Press. 2005.

"Telethon." *Parks and Recreation*. Season 2, Episode 21. May 10, 2010.

Rouse, Josh. "Residential Fishing Licenses up 40% in Kansas through October as Pandemic Continues." *Dodge City Daily Globe*. November 13, 2020.

Outdoor Foundation. 2019-Special-Report-on-Fishing_RBFF_FINAL1.pdf (outdoorindustry.org).

Chapter 2

Smith, Walker. "How to quickly and safely clean your livewells." Wired2fish.com. August 9, 2019. https://www.wired2fish.com/boats-trucks-electronics/how-to-quickly-and-safely-clean-your-livewells/.

"Rules are rules: The dead fish penalty." Bassmaster.com. January 4, 2016. https://www.bassmaster.com/bernie-schultz/rules-are-rules-dead-fish-penalty.

Chapter 3

Schadegg, Andrew. "How to fish a swim jig for bass." Luckytacklebox.com. https://www.luckytacklebox.com/blogs/fishing-tips/how-to-fish-a-swim-jig-for-bass.

Cypress Bend Resort. http://www.cypressbend.com/.

Watson, Jimmy. "Exclusive: Bassmaster names Toledo Bend No. 1 Again." *Shreveport Times*. June 20. 2016.

Toledo Bend fishing records. https://www.toledo-bend.com/toledo-bend/records/.

"TPWD Launches Innovative Bass Tracking Study." *The Katy News*. July 20, 2020.

Carter Carrier

Macaluso, Joe. "Check out fishing results Louisiana B.A.S.S…" Theadvocate.com. October 6, 2019. https://www.theadvocate.com/baton_rouge/sports/outdoors /article_31a3e888-ff6f-11e9-96b0-e761e65c26a9.html.

Chapter 4

Sealock, Jason, and Ryan DaChaine. "What bass look like on down and side imaging." *Wired2fish.com*. June 13, 2016. https://www.wired2fish.com /electronics-tips/what-bass-look-like-on-down-and-side-imaging/.

Wired2fish editors. "8 uses for Humminbird 360 imaging." Wired2fish.com. June 20, 2014. https://www.wired2fish.com/electronics-tips/8-uses-for -humminbird-360-imaging/.

Thermocline

Murray, John. "Fishing the thermocline." Midwestoutdoors.com. June 22, 2020. https://midwestoutdoors.com/fishing-the-thermocline-line/.

Chapter 5

Reel Kids Casting. https://www.bassfederation.com/tbf-youth/reel-kids-casting -competitions/.

Home Improvement. Performance by Tim Allen. 1991–1999.

The Horse Whisperer. Directed by Robert Redford. Performances by Robert Redford and Kristin Scott Thomas. 1998. Film. https://www.imdb.com/ title/tt0119314/.

Largemouth pigment

Hanson, Debbie. "What color is your largemouth bass?" Takemefishing.org. February 3, 2014. https://www.takemefishing.org/blog/february-2014/what -color-is-your-largemouth-bass/.

Coeur D'Alene Records. Certified Weight Fish Records | Idaho Fish and Game.

Trail of the Coeur D'alenes. https://parksandrecreation.idaho.gov/parks/trail-coeur -d-alenes.

Reese, Margaret. "10 tips to learn anatomy + physiology." Medicalsciencenavigator .com. https://www.medicalsciencenavigator.com/10-tips-for-how-to-learn -anatomy-physiology/.

Oraby, Nadine. "Do fish have tongues? Do they have taste buds?" Fluffyplanet .com. 2020. https://fluffyplanet.com/do-fish-have-tongues/.

Chapter 6

Bjanrndottir, Adda. "How much vitamin D should you take for optimal health?" Healthline. June 4, 2017.

Richardson, Miles. "Nature: a new paradigm for well-being and ergonomics." Pubmed.gov. March 22, 2016. https://pubmed.ncbi.nlm.nih.gov/26910099/.

Reynaud's Disease

"Raynaud's Disease." Mayoclinic.org. https://www.mayoclinic.org/diseases -conditions/raynauds-disease/symptoms-causes/syc-20363571.

Esposito, Lisa. "A patient's guide to Rayaud's Syndrome." Usnews.com. December 23, 2019. https://health.usnews.com/conditions/raynauds-syndrome.

Economics

Mileage rate 2020. IRS issues standard mileage rates for 2020 | Internal Revenue Service.

Poverty level. 2020 Poverty Guidelines | ASPE (hhs.gov).

Bettis. Leland. "How much money does a professional fisherman make?" Sapling.com. https://www.sapling.com/12059720/much-money-professional -tournament-fisherman-make.

Chapter 7

Deveau, Jenni et. al. "Improved vision and on-field performance in baseball through perceptual learning." Current Biology. February 14, 2014. https: //www.cell.com/current-biology/fulltext/S0960-9822(14)00005-0.

Computer Vision Syndrome

https://www.medicalnewstoday.com/articles/computer-vision-syndrome #causes.

"Computer Vision Syndrome." AOA.org.

https://www.aoa.org/healthy-eyes/eye-and-vision-conditions/computer -vision-syndrome?sso=y.

Adunka, Oliver. "What you need to know about earbuds and hearing loss." Wexnermedical.osu.edu. January 23 2018.

Hemberlin, Jeremy. "Training your brain to improve your vision." *The Atlantic.* February 19, 2014. https://www.theatlantic.com/health/archive/2014/02/training-your-brain-to-improve-your-vision/283933/.

Chapter 8
Sound Underwater

Lamb, Robert. "How underwater sound systems work." Howstuffworks.com. https://electronics.howstuffworks.com/gadgets/audio-music/underwater-sound-systems.htm.

"Are bass hearing you?" Bassfishingandcatching.com. https://www.bassfishingandcatching.com/bass-hearing.html.

H. Neely Henry spillway schedule. https://apcshorelines.com/our-lakes/neely-henry/.

Drain Santee Cooper?

Alani, Hannah. "Life at SC's lakes Marion and Moultrie is peaceful—unless Santee Cooper folds." *Postandcourier.com.* October 2, 2018. https://www.postandcourier.com/news/life-at-scs-lakes-marion-and-moultrie-is-peaceful-unless-santee-cooper-folds/article_689e313c-d639-11e8-8152-53d5296db372.html.

South Carolina Fishing Records. SCDNR—Freshwater Game Fish Records for SC.

Versatility skills.

Kaplan, Jeremy. "Skillswitching—5 ways to boost your versatility in any field." Careerpro.com. December 20, 2016. https://www.careerpro.com/skillswitching-5-ways-boost-versatility-field/.

Luca, Michael and Bazerman, Max. "Want to make better decisions? Start experimenting." *MIT Management Review.* June 4, 2020.

"How improv methods from comedy can lift business performance." knowledge@wharton. April 9, 2017.

Chapter 9

Eichstead, Michael. "Bass Thumb—Painful Sign of a Good Day." Awesome Mitten.

Baurotrauma

Moody, Ryan. "Releasing fish with barotrauma." Ryanmoodyfishing.com. https://www.ryanmoodyfishing.com/releasing-fish-with-barotrauma/.

Eberts, Rebecca. "Response of Walleye to barotrauma relief treatments . . ." *Journal of Fish and Wildlife Management*. June 2018. https://www.researchgate .net/publication/325659254_Responses_of_walleye_to_barotrauma _relief_treatments_for_catch-and-release_angling_short-term_changes_to _condition_and_behavior.

National Park Service. Catch and Release Fishing—Fish & Fishing (U.S. National Park Service) (nps.gov).

May, Glenn. "Four Offensive Factors." Bassresource.com. March 12, 1999.

Chapter 10

Gladwell, Malcolm. *Outliers*. Little, Brown & Company, 2008.

DeFiori, John et. al. "Overuse injuries and burnout in youth sports." *British Journal of Sports Medicine*. Volume 48. Issue 4. 2013.

Canulette, Andrew. "Bryan College building for success." Bassmaster.com. August 3, 2019.

Chapter 11

Kahneman, Daniel. *Thinking Fast and Slow*. Farrar, Straus & Giroux. 2011.

Alabama Freshwater Fishing Records. State Record Freshwater Fish | Outdoor Alabama.

Jasper. https://alabamanewscenter.com/2018/02/26/jasper-jewel-polished-alabama/

Duncan Bridge Marina Watercolor. https://scottercolors.com/wp-content/uploads /2018/06/DuncanBridgeMarina.jpg.

Barrett, Morag. "What exactly is the mentor's role? What is the mentee's?" *Association for Talent Development*. January 21, 2014.

Chapter 12

"The first five rods every bass fisherman needs." Tacticalbassin.com. November 18, 2015.

Chapter 13

Whitledge, Gregory W., Robert S. Hayward, and Charles F. Rabeni. "Effects of Temperature on Specific Daily Metabolic Demand and Growth Scope of

SubAdult and Adult Smallmouth Bass." *Journal of Freshwater Ecology* 17:3, 353–361. 2002.

Tennessee Fishing Records. State Records | Tennessee Fishing Guide – 2020 | eRegulations.

Chapter 14

Willson, M. *The Music Man*. Performance by Broderick, M.

Idol, B., and James, T. "Dancing with Myself." Performed by Idol, B. Chrysalis. 1981.

APPENDIX II:
Bass Clubs

Local clubs for the lakes covered in this book are listed below:
Toledo Bend area:
https://bassfishingla.com/district-3

Coeur D'Alene area:
https://www.idaho-pba.com/copy-of-2019-results
https://www.westernbass.com/clubs/

Santee Cooper area:
http://www.bassboatcentral.com/bassclubs15.htm

Lake Louis Smith area:
http://www.bhambassclub.org/

Chickamauga area:
http://tnbass.com/clubs.php

The following are some of the bigger club listings from Florida and Texas:
Florida:
https://bassonline.com/florida-fishing-clubs/
http://www.flbasstournaments.com/Bass-Clubs2.html

Texas has some of the oldest bass clubs in the country with several approaching
their diamond anniversary years.
https://www.fishexplorer.com/tx/clubs.asp

The Missouri clubs are close to my heart:
https://innsbrookfishingclub.com/
http://www.mobass.com/content.php?s=fa869fa9673ba63cac09d2720d234fe2

The following is one of the most comprehensive listings of bass clubs:
http://www.bassdozer.com/bass_clubs.shtml

APPENDIX III:
Bass Fishing Journal
Entry (Sample)

Date: _____June 15, 2018_____

Time Period: _____6a until 11a_____

Location: _____Uplake_____

Conditions

Air Temperature: _____75_____

Water Temperature: _____68_____

Weather Conditions: ___Overcast___

Water Conditions: _____Stained_____

Results

Largest fish: ___2 lbs, 4 oz___

Quantity of fish: _____8_____

Lure Selection

Worked: _____Bream deep-diving crank bait_____

Did Not Work: ___Red plastic worm – Texas rigged___

Structure

Target Areas: _____Main lake side ledges_____

Patterns: _____Suspending near rock faces_____

Analysis

Do Again: _____Pause after aggressive first crank_____

Don't Do Again _____Green swim jig_____

Bass Fishing Journal Entry

Date:_____

Time Period:_____until_____

Location: _____

Conditions

Air Temperature:_____

Water Temperature:_____

Weather Conditions:_____

Water Conditions:_____

Results

Largest fish: _____

Quantity of fish: _____

Lure Selection

Worked: _____

Did Not Work: _____

Structure

Target Areas: _____

Patterns: _____

Analysis

Do Again: _____

Don't Do Again _____

Index

Acknowledgments

This book would not have been possible without the support of Emily Harley from the Bassmaster media organization. Emily helped me connect with professional anglers, and she worked behind the scenes to keep the anglers and the organization engaged in the publication.

Melinda Hays gave generously of her time to provide background information for *Next-Level Bass Fishing*. Her insights into the development of collegiate angling were invaluable. In addition, her perspective on the fishing community as well as her sense of the economics of the sport guided this work. I cannot thank her enough.

Julie Ganz and her team at Skyhorse have made the process of converting the manuscript into a finished book smooth and collaborative. Without her passion for the project, *Next-Level Bass Fishing* would not have taken its final form. Kai Texel and Kirsten Dalley contributed their talents to cover and production elements, respectively.

My fishing partner Kurt Dikkers launched this book with a testimonial that was so kind and so complimentary that it was beyond any friend's right to expect. He was an insightful adviser on this project. The professionals might catch bigger bass than Kurt, but no one catches more.

Without Bob Shuman, *Next-Level Bass Fishing* would never have started. His willingness to recenter a fishing book writer away from a troubled novel and back to his sportsman's passions made this book possible.

Jim Spellmeyer has encouraged my writing while being a good and gentle editor. Thanks also to Lily Kinnison, my resident grammarian and wordsmith.

JOURNAL NOTES

JOURNAL NOTES

JOURNAL NOTES

JOURNAL NOTES

JOURNAL NOTES